1970

Christian Art in Africa and Asia

Arno Lehmann

Christian Art in Africa and Asia

With 282 Illustrations

Translators:
Erich Hopka
Jalo E. Nopola
Otto E. Sohn

Concordia Publishing House

Saint Louis   London

A translation of *Afroasiatische christliche Kunst*, by Arno Lehmann
Published 1966 by Evangelische Verlagsanstalt GmbH, Berlin

Licensed English Edition
First published 1969
Library of Congress Catalog Card No. 68-20840
Printed in East Germany
Concordia Publishing House, St. Louis, Missouri
Concordia Publishing House Ltd., London, E. C. 1

English Edition
Dedicated to
Concordia Seminary, Saint Louis, Missouri
in gratitude for the degree
Doctor of Divinity

Contents

The Art of the Others

This book is intended to serve as a companion volume to *Die Kunst der Jungen Kirchen*, Berlin, 1955; 2d ed., 1957 (The Art of the Younger Churches). Its modest objective is the same as that of the volume that preceded it—to present and to give greater publicity to some of the things that "painters, wood-carvers, and architects have begun to achieve in the younger churches," as one review put it in 1958.[1]

The above-mentioned volume has shown and documented when these achievements first began. Since its publication the age of those achievements in art has been heavily underscored by the many accounts and illustrations in the imposing work *Namban Art, Christian Art in Japan, 1549–1639*, by the Japanese Tei Nishimura. The works of Arnulf Camps and Felix zu Löwenstein (see Bibliography) did this also for India under the Great Mogul emperors.

Die Kunst der Jungen Kirchen marked the first attempt in German literature to present a welcome but necessary insight, as we thought, into church art in a more general way. It was designed for those who take part in the life of the church and for those who are devoted to art and have a special interest in it. This second volume constitutes a new attempt. It is being undertaken in the belief that today more than ever before one must keep his eye on the whole world also in the field of art. This second undertaking appears possible and even seems required especially in view of the fact that the initial achievements in artistic endeavor have been carried forward and have found enrichment in the framework of ecumenicity.

This volume, which presents new pictures, furnishes evidence that the work has made progress and invites the reader to look at the pictures and offer his comments. In the final analysis this is very important, no matter whether one likes or dislikes the pictures and no matter what judgments he may feel compelled to make. This request for comments is directed not only to church groups but also to art circles. In spite of the favorable and wide reception of the first volume, which has not lacked expected and just criticism, the art of the ecumenical scene covered by it has remained an almost unexplored field of knowledge. We could hardly expect it to be otherwise. Only gradually will improvements take place by further patient references to those former creators of art and to their achievements, which are so significant for the church and for art in general. When it comes to ecumenical art, a grotesque sight meets our eyes. Many of our contemporaries, in spite of their erudition, in spite of their knowledge of art in other countries, and in spite of their insistence on keeping the whole world in mind and considering its totality, show that they are still pinioned by ideas that reach back almost into the Middle Ages. To them Christian art still seems to be European-Western art exclusively, as if the world had never gotten any larger, as if there were no universal church that crosses the boundaries of nations and races, and as if we were still permitted to live and think in a nonglobal fashion. Dr. John Butler, whose fruitful and stimulating activity becomes evident from the Bibliography, may be right when he says that the West cannot be fair to itself in such a real "conspiracy of silence" and that it must be prevailed upon to forsake its "provincial atmosphere."[2]

This challenge is to be directed first of all to the churches, their leaders and members. It is true that many were pleased with the service the first book rendered; they had been enriched, blessed, and had their horizon broadened by gaining an insight into the art of ecumenicity, perhaps for the first time. Also the Christian press of various countries and languages has carried articles and pictures. Books and encyclopedias, too, have mentioned the art of the younger churches and given space to it for the first time. Thus the first picture shown by the *Weltkirchenlexikon* (Encyclopedia of World Churches), col. 76, is a full-page reproduction of an African "Return of the Prodigal Son." Then, too, it is a distinct pleasure to find that several filmstrips have been prepared for showing at evening meetings; the churches can now see in another way how vast and real the church truly is. It is gratifying and impressive to note also that Christmas and New Year's cards with pictures of ecumenical art are now being made available in several countries. They have had a double effect: the customary cards, which are spiritless and often say nothing, are being shoved off the market, and the person who receives one of these novel cards which have a real message will look at it, examine it, and may even save it. All such tokens of recognition and promotion have been gratefully acknowledged.

There is no question about it: things have improved in this respect. However, the progress made so far is still not entirely adequate, and we must not be satisfied too quickly. Under the influence of ecumenicity, and before that of the missions themselves, the extent of introversion has become less, but still too much of it has remained. In spite of all that has been written and said, it must be observed that the church, and the individual Christian as well, has an inborn inclination toward this stimulating and disturbing movement. The tendency to introversion has developed in an almost uncanny way and, in spite of the many attacks upon it, knows how to maintain itself. Time and time again each one seeks "his own interest" and goes his own way. Also (or even?) the individual Christian must be urged and led with a constant and fresh approach to a new viewpoint and, in many cases, to a change in his course of action. It is significant, quite understandable, and also somewhat embarrassing that the New Testament has put the classic statement "Let each of you look not only to his own interests but *also* to the interests of others" (Phil. 2:4) right in front of that great passage in Philippians which begins with the majestic words, "Have this mind among yourselves, which you have in Christ Jesus." The New English Bible, which has become a best seller, says: "You must look to each other's interest and not *merely* to your own." That's the standard! With its redemption the

10

new creature has acquired the possibility of becoming less self-centered and of finding a solution to the introversion problem.

There is still another person who is worth noting and achieves something. This other person does not enter the picture as a troublemaker in his own ranks but as a representation, an object lesson, and a challenge to us to become aware of today's other art. Viewed from this angle, it is regrettable that even in the geographical vicinity of the author there are still Christian periodicals that have never given their readers even a single example of the art described in this book. Instead, without exception they take their illustrations exclusively from European art, as if nothing had happened in other parts of the world. This is comparable to a theological faculty conducting a workshop on 20th-century art and limiting the field of vision strictly to the boundaries of Europe. The bibliographies, both in the first and in the present volume, show that plenty of published materials, including filmstrips, would be available.

On Nov. 26, 1958, Frank Wesley, an Indian artist with a good reputation, wrote from America: "It is a hard struggle to make a living as a painter." In our day, where can one find patrons who will support these workers in a new territory with a younger and predominantly small and poor church? So far nothing has happened to change an opinion expressed earlier, that in the promotion of artists the Evangelical church is lagging far behind the Roman Catholic sister church. To cite just one example: A musical bulletin has been published in Allahabad, India, since 1960; and within the confines of the apostolic see of India there is a Commission on Indian Art, which for the first 10 years of its existence (until a few years ago) was under the direction of the apostolic prefect, Msgr. J. M. Malenfant, O. F. M. Cap., the bishop of Banaras. The published report of the All India Study Week held in Madras[3] in December 1956 reveals how things are done there. Unfortunately, according to information from the apostolic prefect, no more meetings of this kind have been arranged. In Switzerland, too, the Catholics have had an Association of Christian Architects for Missions since April 1, 1957, because in the areas of the younger churches no one liked to see any more improvised and nonprofessional construction take place. Experts whose names have become household words and young talented architects registered. "In countless spare-time and evening hours" they rendered a valuable service "for the sake of God's reward."[4]

The Evangelical church has done nothing that might be compared with this effort. But it is gratifying to record that the International Union of Bible Societies was concerned with the problem of Bible illustrations at its September 1959 meeting in Edinburgh and saw to it that the Christian art of Asia and Africa would not be ignored in the Bible editions prepared for these continents. The union commissioned the author to assume charge of an Afro-Asiatic section of an exhibit. It was not difficult to write down the names of about 150 artists and budding creators of art in many countries whose addresses were known. And the result? It seemed that they were just waiting for such an encouraging announcement. The number of pictures that arrived in Edinburgh for the proposed texts and themes was a pleasant surprise. A painter from Ghana and one from India were awarded prizes, and another from India received honorable mention. It was learned later that at least in several cases this art fair had also been a factor in securing orders for works

11

of art. The Edinburgh report, which dealt with the problem of Afro-Asiatic illustrations for the Bible and which was in great demand and published in several countries, had also contributed to this happy result.[5] It should be remembered with gratitude that the Committee on World Literacy and Christian Literature ("Lit-Lit") conducts contests for World Christian Art Christmas Cards and offers a prize of one hundred dollars to each winner.[6] Also, in India an *Indian Art Series* is being published.[7] The varied assortment of pictures in the journal of the World Council of Christian Education is also making a far-reaching impact.[8] This council also had an art exhibit in connection with its July 1962 session in Belfast. Youngsters up to 14 years of age from every country in the world were invited to submit their original works of art on the following proposed themes: The Creation, Joseph and His Brothers, Jacob Sends His Sons to Egypt, Psalm 104, Let the Children Come to Me, The Lord's Prayer, The Prodigal Son, The Last Supper, Palm Sunday, The Crucifixion, and The Resurrection. Even if the results of the children's efforts should have been less than had been hoped for, which is open to question, the attempt itself was nonetheless laudable. Perhaps through it the germs of an idea were sown that might not sprout until later on in life. At any rate, future talents have now been directed to Biblical motifs.

It seems particularly important to note that the East Asia Christian Conference was prompted by the printed Edinburgh report to pay greater attention than it had before to illustrating the Bible for its large territory. The author was asked to prepare a book in English depicting paintings by Asiatic artists.

As far as can be determined, the endeavors of the agencies mentioned constitute the only Evangelical activity in this field. In the 40 years of its existence the International Council for Missions (integrated into the Ecumenical Council of Churches in 1961) has not developed any real leadership in the field of art nor given any impulse or even some stimulation to it. The one exception was the 1938 exhibit in Tambaram, which, however, is not mentioned even once in the 7-volume report on its work. Unfortunately no exhibit of the "Art of Ecumenicity" was held at the third plenary meeting of the Ecumenical Council of Churches at New Delhi in 1961. On the other hand the Roman church has sponsored several important exhibits: in 1956 at Utrecht on "Negro Art and Christianity," in 1957 at Recklinghausen, and not long ago in India at St. Anselm College in Ajmer. Visitors came in droves to see the more than 400 paintings and sketches of the leading Catholic artists in India. In Japan the Evangelical groups held an exhibit of Christian art in the Christian House in Osaka.[9]

However, New Delhi did not schedule such an event in 1961, which could have meant much not only to the creating artists but also to the visitors from all over the world, among them individuals with means. And so the art "of the other people" was not to be seen here. Ample encouragement had been given in letters and in print, too, for holding such an exhibit, which would have increased the ecumenical awareness of the viewers and multiplied their joy in belonging to a worldwide church. In 1959 the author said in Edinburgh: "I have often asked myself whether it might not be a very fitting task for the World Council of Churches in Geneva to get the artists together, look after them, and even give them some assistance. This could perhaps be done in conjunction with the International Council for Missions and the International Union of Bible Societies. The main thing is that something be done. Is anyone thinking of exhibiting Christian art of India and Asia and displaying it at the 1961 convention of the World Council of Churches in New Delhi? Why not? Seeing the 'variety of brushes' could carry more ecumenical weight than listening to a new oratorical feat from the variety of silver-tongued theologians."[10]

The patrons of these Christian creators of art in the younger churches must naturally be the mission societies that had participated in the establishment of these churches and which to this day still remember them with all manner of fraternal aid. It has been demonstrated that the missions themselves, as well as their churches in the mother country, are relatively easy to approach and are quite generous when it comes to sacred music. But it is an entirely different matter when pictorial art in involved. There are several Evangelical schools for wood-carvers and painters; more will be said about them later. But they were founded and promoted, to my knowledge, by English missionaries and missions. Except for the one in Neuendettelsau, no German society has ever been known to lend a helping hand in this area. In fact not a single painting by an artist from their fields of activity is known to have been displayed in the meeting rooms of the societies. And so they have missed an opportunity to recognize either a budding or an arrived artist and to promote the cause of native art. Artists want to live, too! It would be the natural thing to display a painting of an African Christ or of Jesus sending out the disciples according to Matthew 28 (see print 34 by an artist from Ghana) in the hall where a society actively engaged in Africa conducts its meetings. The artistic talents are there, they are crying for orders, and a wide assortment is available. An expenditure for such a memento of their work from a church that now has become self-sustaining should be considered proper indeed.

The earnest admonition to leave the "provincial atmosphere" behind is to be addressed also to the European artists and intellectuals, to the science of art, and to the art institutes. The "conspiracy of silence" of these Western circles is still more striking; in view of what is involved, it seems almost beyond comprehension. But one knows, and it can be detected in the brochures and in the bookstores, how much the art of foreign countries is advertised. No one interested in art will want to ignore works of art that are often overpowering in their beauty, nor will he want to do without insight and information concerning these, especially since it involves the individual's culture and his ability to take part in discussion. And no one can conceal the fact any longer that in this century Negro art has had a direct influence on Western art and has functioned "as a catalyst."[11]

When reading treatises on art or long articles about it in encyclopedias, a person cannot but note with disappointment that in almost every case the authors leave the reader with the impression that there is scarcely any other art but European. There is only silence, but in the literature about Africa the reader detects at least a note of recognition in the fact that the missionaries and the missions have been reproached for their extensive lack of understanding of art activity in Africa. In this connection it is almost a pleasure to mention that Hans Himmelheber answers just this charge in his *Negerkunst und Negerkünstler* (Negro Art and Negro Artists).[12] He says: "Unfortunately it cannot be denied that some precious African art has been destroyed by the missions—and is still being destroyed today. But the progress of Islamism has affected Negro art in even a more basic way. Christianity itself would permit Negro art to continue, yes, could even fructify it, but Islamism with its prohibitions against figurative imagery is stamping out Negro plastic art completely in its territories." We would of course have liked to see this bare statement supported by some present-day evidence.

But Hans Himmelheber also speaks of a missionary Emonts who "in 1913 had met a chieftain from Babanki and had described him as a first-rate wood-carver." This one example shows that the negative opinions about the missions and missionaries are not and cannot be valid in every case and that the "blind spot" in those men was not so large and their barbarism not so bad as one might be tempted to believe at first in reading some of these reports.

In his *Afrikanische Kunst* (African Art), which appeared in 1960, Boris de Rachewiltz, too, is critical of the older missions, whose "fight against 'paganism'" he characterizes as merciless. It is by no means the intention of Rachewiltz in any way to cast doubt on the genuineness of individual conversions, nor even to question the good faith of the missionaries who, he believes, were convinced they were doing the right thing.[13] Quite justly he then raises his voice against the "stucco saints and faded oleographs," as the Catholics have also done. He knows of the bronze crucifixes from the 16th and 17th centuries and evaluates these objects—but he doesn't say a word about the newer Christian art of Africa.[14] That silence again! In this connection, in a well-chosen bibliography he also mentions Rolf Italiaander's *Neue Kunst in Afrika* (New Art in Africa). In it the author also has some sharp words for "fanatical missionaries" and for "a veritable iconoclastic assault on pagan art" and then says: "It can only be a welcome sight for an art lover to see the problems of Christian art in Africa portrayed so unsparingly even by Christian writers; in fact, it appears the voices of those who recognize all the dangers are multiplying today. Indeed, they are not to be underrated! This in no way implies that the missionaries devoted to art perhaps do not have good intentions. In fact they have very good intentions, but they are laboring under a delusion. However, for the time being no pleasure can in most cases be derived from being obliged to behold what is being accomplished in the various art schools of Africa under church sponsorship. This statement in many cases is far too mild; one should rather have spoken of a betrayal—namely a betrayal of all the principles that apply equally well to culture and religion."[15] We are delighted with these frank words as well as with every honest criticism because, among other things, they at least show how others see us. And they echo our basic concern: an awareness must be created first!

On the other hand, Boris de Rachewiltz could have seen from this valuable booklet that there is in Africa a new Christian art which he failed to mention—no matter what his opinion of it might have been. Rolf Italiaander tells of his "heartening experience" when he had "the opportunity to observe the sensational activity at the Cyrene Mission in Southern Rhodesia," where "the art center was under the direction of that splendid Reverend Edward Paterson for 14 years (since 1939)." At that, Italiaander devotes two pages (20 f.) to the activities there. And above all: Of the

39 pictures he uses to demonstrate the new art, 10 were conceived and done by Christians; the phenomenal plastic work *Slavery* by Benjamin Mensah (print 179) and two wood plastics from the Congo "which clearly reveal the influence of Christianity"[16] must be included, too. Rachewiltz at least could have gotten an initial insight into the variety and the level of achievement of the contributions to African art by Christianity from the book he mentioned, as the title of his own book would suggest. Whether he did or did not, his silence on the matter speaks volumes. This lack of "reference" in African literature "to Christian art, which has been developing for over 50 years," has been noticed and pointed out also by others.[17] How much more realistic by comparison and likewise more useful is the major work *Modern Indian Painting*, put out by a Hindu, which did not pass over the creations of Christian art in silence but included five Christian paintings.[18] Besides criticizing Christian art, the beautiful work *The Sculpture of Africa*[19] also pays tribute to it.

Even though it is true, as has been pointed out, that the history of art has treated (and still does) exotic art like a stepchild,[20] it is hardly possible or very difficult to understand why even Christian writers on art should be inclined to ignore and pass over Christian exotic art in silence. A pleasant exception is Lothar Schreyer, who includes among his 40 illustrations 5 examples from the art of "the others": a native church on Manus, one of the Admiralty islands; a Mary Magdalene from Vietnam; a carved-wood crucifix from Tanzania; an ivory Madonna from the Ivory Coast; and the famous Return of the Prodigal Son, hewn from stone by Sam Songo of Cyrene. In the comments that precede the illustrations he offers suggestions for understanding the respective pictures.[21] Also in the text itself Lothar Schreyer often refers to non-European art[22] and proves that he means what he says in the title of his *Christliche Kunst des XX. Jahrhunderts* (Christian Art in the 20th Century) and that he neither makes nor recognizes geographical limitations.

Another book entitled *Kunst und Kirche im XX. Jahrhundert* (Art and the Church in the 20th Century) provides less satisfaction because it fails to live up to its title, which apparently promises to cover the entire field of church art. In the text, however, there is only one cursory reference to Africa, and in the pictorial section only two offerings from Africa can be found: a colored wood figure (but reproduced in black and white) from Nigeria of St. Francis Preaching to the Birds and a copper engraving, The Denial of St. Peter, from Dahomey.[23] In this case one can indeed say that the title suggested something more. Besides being untenable, it doesn't make sense in today's world for a European to think that the 20th century belongs more or less to him *alone*. The others belong to the 20th century, too, and are in it and—in many ways—very active! It can no longer be taken for granted that 20th-century art is exclusively European or even almost so. If one wishes to deal only with this phase of art, be it in print or speech, it should be indicated in the title or in the theme, for every alert person thinks of and looks for more than only Europe when the 20th century is mentioned. One must take the truth, the world situation, and above all the rights of "the others," which are not inferior to those of a European, into account and consider them in formulating the title of a book. The author should have said "European Art of the 20th Century." The title of the book *Art and the Message of the Church*,[24] for instance, also promises too much; adding "in America" would have told the truth and prevented an Asiatic buyer from becoming disillusioned.

Poiesis,[25] with the subtitle *Theologische Untersuchung der Kunst* (A Theological Investigation of Art), is a book that is really worth reading; but here again one cannot blame a person for becoming amazed and disappointed, too, that "art" once more is being viewed and explored with the foregone conclusion that there is no other art but Western art. Inserting "Western" before "Art" in the subtitle or adding "of Europe" to it could have protected the person with a global taste for art from the illusion that at last he had found in the writer an author who reckons with the reality of today's world and has dared to leap into this expansive sea. But actually in this so fundamental, comprehensive, and valuable treatise, as presented by Bahr in his *Poiesis*, he never mentions anywhere or indicates in any way, directly or indirectly, that there is such a thing as Christian art that is not European. Celso Costantini is mentioned twice in the text but without referring to the art of the younger churches, even though he was the leading figure in demanding and promoting this art.[26] He is not listed in the Bibliography. In connection with such a thorough theological consideration of the nature of Christian art it must have seemed interesting and tempting to go into the problems of interpretation and communication in the field of non-European art and perhaps call attention to the "holy enterprise" of the black "Christ" or of the "Christ" from China or India.

Our concern is a very modest one: we are concerned about the attention being given to the art of "those others" in the non-European world, where it is open to every possible type of criticism. It is not right nor is it good if this art is ignored. When a review of my earlier book on art stated, "This work is an esthetic sensation,"[27] and when it also recommended the book especially to the connoisseurs, we are sure it was done only because it might help them focus their attention on that totality which also embraces the creative art of "the others." This is true even if the viewers should not happen to like the works and come up with very deprecating criticism, expressing it clearly and with polite frankness.

It is not chiefly a matter of recognition and approval; the main thing is the honest recognition and viewing of what else is present. Also at stake is a recognition of the simple fact that many artistic talents are in evidence and do exist, no matter how one might venture to appraise their work as a European.

At no time and in no place, neither in Europe nor in Asia and Africa, has it ever been said or even indicated that Christian Afro-Asiatic art has reached its goal, has served as a typical model, or even attained maximum production. That is still true today—although it can be said in fairness that one does indeed come across good productions and catch sight of works that are good enough to be shown and would find a good spot and recognition at a European exhibit. It must be remembered, too, that the output and variety are not insignificant: thousands of pieces of Christian art come from those two continents. We have already mentioned the art fair in Ajmer, India, with its more than 400 exhibits. This brings to mind other Catholic exhibits noted for their wealth of works that surely must have been of varying caliber. The Chinese Shek-kai-nung (Johnny Shek) has painted hundreds of Biblical pictures. The Catholic artist from India, Angelo Da Fonseca, wrote me on Aug. 18, 1960, that he could not remember the exact number of pictures he had painted, "but it must be more than 500, of which perhaps less than 50 were done in oil and the rest in water-color." When we hear of his productivity, even only in part, as must necessarily be the case with us, then we can well understand why a kind voice has called him the father, yes, even "the patri-arch of Christian art in India."[28]

If someone should ask how this blind spot can be accounted for in those who in general and as Christians are interested in art, its creation, and its problems a few partial answers may be offered. Many people, also Christians, have not been informed that there actually *is* such a thing as Christian Afro-Asiatic art. This information has not reached the people in the church services, in church meetings and reports, or through church periodicals. This may be partly their own fault for not looking around and for failing to look at the literature, the catalogs, and the publication notices. And unquestionably there are also those who live without a church and have never known that there are churches literally in every country of the world. Then, too, we find others who make a pretense of Christianity or profess a dubious kind of benevolent and neutral "churchliness." These exhaust themselves mostly with extraneous matters and never enter through a church door or rarely glance at Christian literature. No wonder they have no knowledge of the world and are not willing to think in universal terms or to live with a globe in front of their face. The result is obvious: He who is not thoroughly familiar with the big garden will not recognize the various fruits and flowers that grow in it.

It is therefore important to remember that even in those areas which are receptive to variety and change the right method to approach exotic art in a scientific manner has still not been found, neither is it known how it is really absorbed. For exotic art is completely in a class by itself and belongs to a wholly different and self-contained world of thought and perception. Here one en-counters something that is not easy to classify and fit into a pattern. Nevertheless, even such a difficulty can be overcome. Of course, in the event that "the criteria according to which the artistic degree of a work is to be measured are as valid in every way for it (Christian art) as for Western art,"[29] it then appears to us the question is still in order whether these criteria should be applied too hastily. The warning of Eliot Elisofon against rash and overly crictical considerations from an artistic point of view is very much in place here, because through these hasty judgments an "opaque wall of separation consisting mostly of a torrent of irrelevant words"[30] is erected be-tween the work and the viewer. This warning would apply not only to the African sculptural art, which is "ultimately nondescriptive in character." But in any case it may be true here, too, that haste makes waste. It may take years for us to feel our way into the art of others and to develop the insight that is dependent entirely on the viewer's empathy. What an Indian said when the exhibit "5000 Years of Art from India" was opened at Essen in 1959 is still valid: "Appreciation for art, especially for that from a completely different climate and from another environment, requires a bit of effort, much imagination, and even more empathy. Not understanding a thing is often not the fault of the thing itself but is due to one's own inability."[31]

These words must be kept in mind even more when we deal with a hitherto unknown Christian art. It is almost impossible to get at it with the usual criteria of art, especially if they are hastily applied. This kind of art demands more from the viewer. Without like-mindedness there can be no comprehension or understanding! Without this—shall we call it congeniality?—we shall never get beyond the waiting room. The test can be made without going beyond the confines of Europe. We are thinking of the unusually daring, modern illustrations of the Bible and of the missal of Frère Yves and that of Frère Jacques.[32] Or the unusual and beautiful book of the latest Bible illustrations in England might be mentioned; at first Noël van Alphen's Biblical illustrations are often shocking to Englishmen accustomed to the old picture content.[33] All of these new Biblical illustrations may not immediately please everyone, and that applies also to those who fully understand their artistic value. They will not unfold at the mere sound of explanations, but they will reveal themselves to the congenial viewer, the observant eye, and the devout heart. We are saying all this in connection with the presentation of the pictures in this book, not only because we are concerned about pointing out a hitherto neglected corner in the vast garden of art, but also and above all because besides recognition we are concerned about a deep understanding of this art and the artists. We invite the reader to look, to look and draw his own conclusions.[34] For this reason we have no intentions of explaining the pictures. Steinhausen, who called his paintings "my prayers," did not want to explain his either, or have them explained: "Each person has to decide for himself what my pictures have to say to him. I cannot do that for him."[35]

The Other Art

Non-Western art is and must be different. In the process of becoming so, however, it did not remain free of importations from the West, of imitations and borrowings, and of a marked Western influence—all of which led to various heterogeneous forms. The same things occured years earlier in various geographical and cultural areas. In this respect ecclesiastical art in general does not differ from that of her secular sister. That this took place is understandable and could hardly be avoided, and in our day of closer contacts, deeper knowledge, and inevitable exchanges this is especially true, even more often than before.

We are happy over the discovery of African art and its effects on European artists. We should refrain from getting wrought up to any degree because a fructifying to-and-fro and a giving and receiving is going on—all the more so since no one can in any way foretell what the result of such a development will be.

However, such open-mindedness does not set aside the principle and the fact that every artist will strive to labor in the present, among his own people, within his own milieu, and with his own tools and withal to be completely himself, as indeed he must. Hence we can understand and must expect Christian Afro-Asiatic art to have a character all its own, which with all its open-mindedness and readiness to learn it wants to retain. We can tell from the pictures whether it has achieved this purpose and to what degree. It would not have required the services of a critic to point out that nothing final and conclusive had been presented in my first volume on art. If this should be said also about the present volume, let me state here and now that it would meet with our complete approval. When one is required to break new ground and meet a publisher's deadlines for the first time, he cannot do it without using some still unfinished works and without relying on interim reports. The same happens in European circles: We follow the artists step by step, watch over their shoulder as they experiment, and then look forward to what we shall see when the hard struggle is over. The day will come when we may speak about these activities and publish what is of sufficient interest and value to merit the attention of larger circles, invite them also to become a part of this effort, and encourage them to support it.

The items collected by this combined effort could be processed later by experts, who should be better qualified for this task than representatives of the first generation. Someone has said so beautifully that a new (not Western!) "wedding gown must be woven" for the bride of Jesus in every nation "from the particular cultural values that are familiar to that respective nation."[36] Even then, all kinds of flaws may appear, and we shall be able to say for a long time to come —if not always—that the ultimate has not yet really been achieved and that the subject matter, as well as the style and treatment, still has many faults that need correction. No one will be surprised if faults are found. However, no one would want to say we must not look at what has already been accomplished but had better wait until the final and complete product is available. In this connection we must remember above all that, except for the purely professional craftsmen, the painters and carvers of Asia and Africa are often first-generation Christians who after all cannot be expected to have a full and deep Christian understanding of all these things. It was not an outsider but a padre who said: "A Negro really has no idea of what it means to live like a Christian. But what do we really know about the true nature of Christian life? He does not know how to approach it and therefore gives stammering expression to Christian life in crude art." The church in the Western world did not produce a Dürer, a Michelangelo, and a Bach at once, and no one believes that a history of art in Europe would start out with only such names. The Negro now finds himself in the same position as the artist working in Europe: facing "a new beginning."[37] But there are two things that may be said with some degree of certainty. The quantity and the quality of Afro-Asiatic art are greater than first meets the eye, and today's missionaries follow the ambition and work of the artists closely and give them encouragement and support, although we must say that what is given is still inadequate. He who is acquainted with the literature in this field knows that this has not always been the case, and so we should consider such a development as a welcome turn of events for the better.

There was no lack of articulate criticism of earlier attitudes and activities. For good reasons the candid words of Father F. van Trigt, S.M.A., who was quoted earlier, must head the list of only a few examples: "When he (the Negro) turned to Christianity, the bottom fell out of native art. The Christian art that had been brought into the country by Roman Catholic missionaries could have become a new source of religious artistic endeavor if it had been able to find an intellectual rapprochement with Negro art. But we know that this did not happen. The missionaries who started to build churches in the latter half of the past century followed the new Gothic and Romanesque architecture and unleashed a veritable iconoclastic war against pagan art. They had brought with them whole shiploads of European devotional materials for this purpose—pictures that cost little or nothing and which bore no resemblance at all to the art familiar to Negroes."[38] Leon Bloy called these pictures of the saints "inferior representations in poorest taste," and Christoph von Fürer-Haimendorf tells about the "gruesome chromos" of Old Testament scenes that he saw in one church, and then mentions that he even saw a grave decorated with a magazine clipping of Marlene Dietrich.[39] The theologian Thomas Ohm, a Catholic missionary, voices an equally severe criticism. On his extensive travels he saw the many "coffee pictures of the heart of Jesus and of Mary that are found so frequently in the missions ... ['coffee' pictures because they were trash and looked as if coffee had been used instead of paint]. A second glance at the Christian paintings that we have provided for the missions during the various phases of their existence for perhaps a hundred years, readily convinces us that those ancient relics which were supposed to pass for Christian art are of the lowest quality in the entire history of Christian art. The art of the missions definitely contributed to the low state of our Christian art. Yes, it often was even worse than Christian art in Europe. But since that time a desire for an honest and vigorous form has taken hold also in the missions."

A recent Catholic book says with equal frankness: "A conscientious examination of the present situation forces us to admit without further ado that in general the imported Christian art is of a very low artistic quality; actually in all too many cases it simply does not deserve to be called art in any sense whatever. This applies especially to those 'art objects' that are produced in Western plants and then shipped off to the missions. An enormous amount of trash and 'rubbish' has come to us even from countries that have a great Christian tradition."[40]

Christoph von Fürer-Haimendorf knows that the missionaries approached their work "with the best of intentions and filled with high ideals." But he regrets, and justly so, that the ancient art of wood carving, practically the only activity of the Konyak and Ao tribes in the field of pictorial art, had not been employed anywhere in the decoration of churches (opposite p. 105, No. 45, he presents an impressive wood plastic of a dwelling for men) and deplores that the ancient Naga music has become unpopular, that the old designs in men's fabrics have disappeared, and that the opportunities for dancing, which until then had been very closely associated with every festive occasion, have declined.[41]

The artist F. N. Souza of Goa said that not only the Vandals, the Conquistadors, and the Victorians but also the missionaries must be held responsible for destroying the continuity of Indian culture through effective invasion.[42] And it is said in South Africa that the missionaries had done little to create new avenues of expression to satisfy a compelling urge for doing manual art.[43] "They opposed the artistic creations of an ancestral belief with saints of stucco and faded oleographs, so that Rémy de Gourmonts was prompted to say, 'Religious art is dead.'"— B. de Rachewiltz puts it this way, "The pictures of saints . . . do not arouse a great deal of interest in art."[44]

Comments like these should be heeded and not brushed aside hastily, not even when it is felt that the criticism must be qualified somewhat.

The church has no reason for and no intention of concealing, suppressing, or denying the deplorable mistakes that have been made. And the examples that have been mentioned are by no means the only ones. The words of James, "But the wisdom from above . . . is open to reason" (3:17), are applicable also to this situation. One must be ready to listen also to those things that are not always pleasant to hear. Particularly valuable in this instance is the Catholic self-criticism that became evident in the two quotations cited.

But how account for the failure to achieve the intended purpose? With no intention to discount the criticism, we must, in the interest of clarification, point out three things:

First, it must be remembered and acknowledged that the Christian faith is always a novelty wherever it is found and that it and the new standards and values produced by this New Message also act like an unheard-of force that has the capacity to cause a revolutionary upheaval. It is a feature of the new faith that it cannot blindly accept the entire status quo as something self-evident and then carry on from there. Even political systems do not operate in this manner, especially if they think they have something radically new to offer.

Second, besides recognizing this personal commitment, we must also not overlook the special conditions and prevailing ideas of the past if we want to gain a fairly correct understanding of how things were handled then in a given situation. This association with a given period is extremely important. The impression can easily become distorted if this time factor is not taken into consideration and if past accomplishments are compared with today's achievements and then measured with standards that we think are valid. The pioneer missionaries encountered difficult situations: The large number of problems clamoring for attention were all new; not only did they have to acclimate themselves and learn new languages, but in many cases they had to engage in language study first and consolidate the findings into a written language; they often had to make quick decisions without waiting for advice, for mail service was very slow in those days; and besides, who in their distant homeland could have given them expert advice? At first they were so occupied with understanding and mastering the language, which took place only gradually, that they had no time whatever in their busy schedule for supervising all facets of the work, let alone understand every phase of it. And if, for instance, they had to erect churches, perhaps in Africa—the theologians, mind you!—which type of architecture did Africa have to offer and where could they have found guidelines for building suitable native-Christian churches—and architects—in those early days? Which Japanese, Indian, or African builders could have advised them and relieved them of the responsibility for selecting a desirable form of architecture that would result in a house of God and not just any kind of building? The many problems connected with building churches can be seen from the lively discussions that constantly still take place at conferences on church construction, and are also evident in the literature on the subject in the European area.

Third, mistakes have been made even though the reasons for making them could be explained. How delightful it would have been if the correct solutions could have been sought and found right from the beginning. But today many things have changed and improved. Incidentally, it should be remembered that it was missionaries who discovered the designs on the rocks in the vicinity of Lake Victoria (and they didn't even destroy them!).[45] But far more important are the changes in attitude resulting from greater exposure to art, the intention to concentrate on "indigenous art" that is native and permanently rooted to the soil, and the many indications of support for the production of this kind of art. No exact figures for this still inadequate support and production are available. But what has been assembled and made accessible to the public is nevertheless not a very small amount. It includes, among others, *Die Kunst der Jungen Kirchen* and the sundry items in it on the history of this art, the various art exhibits, the great works of Celso Costantini, Sepp Schüller, Daniel Johnston Fleming, and an extensive bibliography that has been updated for this volume. We have already spoken of the art exhibits that have been held recently. F. van Trigt, who we know does not beat around the bush with criticism, made a statement with which perhaps all will agree in principle: "The church that can and will be Greek to the Greeks and barbarian to the barbarians is convinced that genuine Christian art should be developed by the people it has to serve. The church has obligated its missionaries to give the native artists guidance in developing Christian themes, for these artists did not always take up art for art's sake alone but also for economic reasons."[46] Thomas Ohm, the distinguished advocate of research for Catholic missions, agrees with him: Even though the missions were deluged with European art, and quite often "with that of the lowest quality from the 19th and 20th centuries," yet "in the course of time a change of heart had occurred, and men then acted accordingly." "Christianity demands forms of art that are in keeping with its newness and which will make it easy to see its novel features."[47] The following comment did not originate in mission circles and therefore deserves our close attention. Janheinz Jahn states in his book *Muntu*[48] (also available in English translation): "For several years the Catholic Church has tried to use the services of African artists. One of the most successful attempts was undertaken by Father K. Carrol in Oye-Ekiti, Nigeria. He assembled a group of young wood-carvers, who had been trained already in traditional art, and encouraged them to develop Christian themes." Mary acquired a Muntu face! Jahn also speaks very highly of the efforts of Makerere College in Kampala, Uganda, which is trying to find new themes and set new tasks for traditional art in order to bring into being a new form of African art. Samples of these efforts are shown in the picture section of this volume. One of the most productive and most courageous artists, and also the best-known African painter in Europe and in America, is Prof. Sam Ntira from Kampala, who is a Chagga and a member of the Lutheran Church.[49]

Rolf Italiaander also mentions various Christian art schools on African soil. He is convinced that the missionaries do have good intentions, in fact "even the very best of intentions." But he still maintains that "for the time being no pleasure can, in most cases, be derived from being obligated to behold what is being accomplished in the various art schools of Africa under church sponsorship." To call it trash would still be far too mild; one should rather have said betrayal. This is harsh language, and he does not support it with specific proofs or reasons. In any case, his verdict must be toned down a bit; even he knows, of course, that only a beginning has been made and that fruit does not ripen on request. In spite of all the criticism he has to offer, he too refers to the art school that was established in 1937 at Makerere College in Kampala with generosity and appreciation. He also reproduces two pictures and is aware of the great popularity of the pictures from Kampala; the people of Uganda use them as wall decorations because "they are just right for them." He, unlike Jahn, takes his readers also to Cyrene. After his disappointing experiences with other Christian art schools, "the opportunity to observe the sensational activity at the Cyrene Mission in Southern Rhodesia was all the more heartening. This art center was conducted with great skill and success by the Rev. Edward Paterson. This institute, situated 20 miles southwest of Bulawayo, attracts art students not only from Rhodesia but also from Nyasaland, South Africa, Basutoland [Lesotho], Swaziland, and Bechuanaland [Botswana]. And the Church of England can certainly be satisfied with the reputation which the school and its students enjoy. . . . One of the most highly gifted Negro artists in Cyrene is Sam Songo from Belingwe, who now teaches at this school although both of his feet and his right hand are crippled. His painting of the ancient Bantu gold mines and the other oils and watercolors by him are phenomena." On the other hand Songo's sculpture of St. Francis does not elicit praise from Italiaander, for this Francis reminds him too much of "The Kid from Munich" or of a bad liquor advertisement. "And yet in the field of sculpture, which flourishes in some parts of Christianized Negro Africa, there are also works that are captivating—perhaps because 'the Christian forms' are expressed 'in a spluttering way.'" In his book Italiaander has reproduced four good examples, numbers 24—28. And these only, for "we are not presenting any examples of unsuccessful, passionate trash and other Christian-African pseudo art, although if we did, the good examples undoubtedly would produce a still more striking impression."[50]

We are delighted with such words for the simple reason that they not only show an awareness of Christian art but also do not suppress criticism, which is needed by the artists and is an aid to us viewers. Such utterances in literature provide evidence for what I already have called the real concern also of this publication, namely, recognition, some degree of understanding by the general public that non-European Christian art is a part of the entire field of Christian art, and that it is emerging from its "conspiracy of silence." Several short articles give us a deeper insight into the work of the Cyrene Mission and that of Father Kevin Carrol, S.M.A., who was mentioned earlier as being active in Nigeria. The evidence they supply in regard to the work of the missionaries and their ideas about art seem important enough to warrant quoting at length from them.

Carrol discusses the question, "Is it possible to produce Christian art in Africa and Asia?"[51] He answers his own question as follows: "The question has been raised: Why did the bishops in

Africa pay so little attention to Rome's request for the exploitation of native art for Christian themes? Until recently it might have appeared that the new Africa had given up its traditional art. The bishops felt that an adaptation of this art was not the answer to a situation that actually existed in the creation of African art. This in turn led to another question: Would not the revival of this dead or dying art be just another empty exercise in historicism, as was the revival of the Gothic in Europe? Has not Christian art in China and Japan been reproached many times for trying to put new life into the ancient forms that had died long ago when it should have switched to the creation of the modern lively art of today's Asia instead?

"In 1954 two modern churches were completed for the university in Ibadan, a metropolis in the Western Region of Nigeria, one for the Catholics and the other for the Protestants. The wood carvings for the Protestant chapel were ordered from the only Western-trained wood-carver in Nigeria, from a Catholic who got his training in European art academies. The doors of the Catholic chapel were produced by a Moslem wood-carver who uses the traditional forms of Nigeria. Can the church boards therefore be accused of conforming to Rome's wishes prematurely?

"Hardly, for the art of wood carving among the Yorubas in the Western Region of Nigeria is not a dead art. These wood-carvers still have the capacity to adjust to today's new conditions and assignments. According to expert opinion the carved work in the Catholic chapel is of a far higher quality than that in the Protestant building. Besides, it costs only a fraction of the price. It is far beyond our means to employ artists to any great extent who have exaggerated notions about the value of their services. . . .

The Church and African Art

"In 1946 The Society for African Missions started a research center in Oye-Ekiti for the exploitation of Yoruban culture for Christian purposes. At that time there were no educated Africans who might have taken some interest in these problems. Today their number is growing rapidly, also among the expert academicians, who are paying fresh attention to their traditional culture. The public has already been won over to such an extent that it is possible to expend government funds for purchasing works of traditional art to be used as furnishings for public buildings.

"Recently a conference of architects in Nigeria decided to use also African motifs in every modern building. The first modern building on which African forms of art were used appears to have been the university chapel mentioned above. In 1955 our wood-carvers also made the speaker's chair for Parliament and the chair of state for the Council of Chieftains in Ibadan (see illustration on p. 207 of *Catholic Missions*, 1960). We ourselves carved the figures on the episcopal throne for our cathedral in Ibadan. The five double doors of the cathedral were finished in 1957. They were all paid for by Africans, one of the doors being donated by a prominent political figure. In 1958 we completed another big project: We installed the paneling and supplied the decorations for that very fine official residence of the Prime Minister of the Western Region of Nigeria.

24

"Space will not permit us to describe the development and adaptation in the various branches of Nigerian industrial art: weaving, embroidering, bead and leather work. I will also have to omit music. In passing, we can say that this development is not confined only to the traditional techniques. One African nurse, for instance, has learned how to make the traditional style of embroidery on a modern embroidering machine. A young African from an art school has just completed a series of black-and-white and colored illustrations for religious books. The inspiration and feeling they convey are really African.

"Then, too, people have wondered whether this Christian art from Africa may have led to any conversions. I do not think so. But I am convinced that appropriately furnished church buildings and a liturgy, above all, the development of African religious music and poetry, would attract our Africans to church. . . .

"Our work in Oye-Ekiti has been criticized from two entirely different directions. Some believe: 'Without a heathen religion to inspire its production African Christian art will remain sterile.' Others have said: 'Only artists who are Christians can create Christian art.' I wish to say only a few words in reply to both of these criticisms: Both are wrong even though they contain a grain of truth. By referring to the works of three wood-carvers, I will try to present a clear picture of the real situation. The three are Areogun, born around 1880; Bandele, who was born about 1910; and Fakeye, born in 1930. Areogun was a heathen; his son Bandele is a nominal Catholic; and Fakeye, Bandele's pupil, is a Moslem.

Areogun, the Heathen

"He died in 1952 at an age of about 70 years. He was one of the great wood-carvers. He came from a region where Yoruban wood carving was in full bloom. He was no 'savage,' a prey of myth and fear, but a venerable and discerning old man. He carved various figures and masks for me in the traditional style. As subjects he used kings, hunters, women, and children from the village life as he knew it. I have found samples of his work within a radius of 30 miles. Like most of the carved works of the Yorubas, the productions of Areogun, too, were creations of a judge of human nature who accurately noted each detail of the everyday life around him and knew how to capture it in wood. Even when he carved things for the worship of idols, he did so with the same true-to-life style. European collectors of African art prefer the more conventional and abstract works of other regions and so perhaps have missed an opportunity to note the Yoruban art, for the Yoruba country is one of the richest sources of wood carvings in Africa. I do not want to maintain that religion had no influence on Areogun whatever. This influence was still strong enough to distinguish his work from that of the average human life. However, the inspiration for his art did not come from some kind of mystical contact with spirits, ancestors, or forces of nature, as some authors from Africa like to imagine. An intimate knowledge of people is what makes it possible for Yoruban wood-carvers to adjust to new conditions without losing their creative vigor.

"Bandele is the son of Areogun. He grew up when a money economy, trucks, and imported goods appeared on the scene. He calls himself a Catholic because he attends our church now and then and sends his children to our school. He started to work for me in 1947. Before this he had worked in the same style and in about the same area of subject matter as his father Areogun. To begin with, I asked him to carve a mother of God and her child for me. For this he abandoned the compact architectural style and the way in which traditional Yoruban art approaches its subject matter. It seems he had tried to copy a European figure, although to my knowledge no such figures were to be seen in that area. Then I commissioned him to carve Nativity figures and requested him to begin with the three Magi. I asked him to carve these in the same style that he used for the royal figures on the porch doors of the chieftain palaces. So these figures had the compact style that I had expected, and he had no further difficulty in doing Mary and Joseph in the same way. When he asked me how Mary and Joseph were to be dressed, I referred him to several Catholics. They told him to dress them like priests and nuns but with a cord around the waist and a halo on their head. He did not ask what kind of clothing the other persons wore but carved them in the traditional Yoruban dress. Bandele did not even ask whether some persons were to be represented as Africans or Europeans. Probably he thought he was carving Europeans; be that as it may, it hardly makes any difference in their appearance. It has often been said that Africans do not like to see sacred personages represented as Africans. This could be an acquired reaction, since all the religious pictures and statues they get to see portray the European type. When this question arises, I always tell them, 'Jesus was not a European but a Syrian.' And of course they have often seen Syrian storekeepers. By the way, all the illustrations used in the advertisements by newspapers and publications present African types.

Fakeye, the Moslem

"Fakeye, the third artist, comes from a family of wood-carvers. He was sent to school before he had completed his training as a carver. After his school days were over, he began to teach the art of wood carving in a trade school. I sent him to Bandele for a 3-year apprenticeship. Shortly before this his parents had turned Moslem. He calls himself by the Moslem name of Lamidi and fasts during Ramadan, the lunar month in which Moslems abstain from food. Most of the projects which we completed since 1954 were carried out by Fakeye and his assistants and apprentices. One example will suffice to demonstrate the extent of his activities. Early last year we felled three iroko trees which we then cut up into six logs about 13 feet long. In nine months practically all the wood was used up. We carved some of the logs into traditionally designed columns for the Jos Museum, from the rest we made the Stations of the Cross for the university chapel at Ibadan, the figures on the episcopal throne in the cathedral, and various other items.

"Christian art by a non-Christian artist?

"Someone is sure to ask, 'How can a Mohammedan carver create Christian works of art?' But he actually does. Of course, we cannot expect him to have the deep religious feeling of perhaps a Fra Angelo. However, events in the life of our Lord can be portrayed in a simple, decorative manner. There is no reason why a Moslem or heathen could not create such a work out of genuine respect for Christ and His mother. Moreover, the portraiture of a person's character and his inner feelings is somewhat unusual in Yoruban art. To demand that our carvers express character and emotion would be asking too much from the abilities of our people. Such endeavors should be reversed for well-trained artists.

"In his *Muntu, an Outline of Neo-African Culture*, Janheinz Jahn attempts to estimate the value of our efforts. I have met Jahn. However, I found the 'ethereal way' in which he looks at things very difficult to understand. He was shocked at my 'materialistic' attitude when I observed that the art of carving should pay its way if it was to survive. To Jahn, African art is something sacred. But sacred or not, the carvers won't carve without some form of suitable compensation. The name Areogun really means: he who earns money in serving Ogun. Ogun is the god of those who use tools and weapons made of iron. Jahn was disappointed, too, that our carvers must of necessity work in a framework of strictly geometric proportions. The spontaneous forms of the past are more to his liking. But at present the architects simply insist on accurate measurements and straight edges. Our artists must either comply with these terms or starve. ...

"Jahn's criticism is interesting but pointless and without foundation. How can he tell whether the quality of Christian art has deteriorated when there is no way of comparing it with African production in general. ... I, in turn, could produce many examples of pagan works of far inferior artistic value. ...

"A closer study of Yoruban culture and religion will enable us to understand why someone who is not convinced of the objective validity of Christianity can allow himself to be carried away by the beauty of pagan worship. ...

"About all the missionaries can accomplish is to begin on the work of preserving the values of 'Negro culture' and blending these values with Christianity. The completion of this work, namely, the creation of a Christian African culture and of an African Christianity, will be the task of the native church in Africa, its African bishops, priests, and faithful."

An illustrated pamphlet by Rev. E. G. Paterson tells us about Cyrene.[52] A motion picture has been made about Cyrene; the film *Pitaniko* presents the life of the missionaries and the activities of the art school and its chief figure, crippled Sam Songo, who has been mentioned before.[53] A catalog of an exhibit of Bantu art was put out with the title *Cyrene and Its Art*. It states: "The works of the students at Cyrene have been found all over the world. The royal family owns 6 of these paintings and carved works. A large collection went to America, and a second exhibit from Cyrene is being circulated throughout England under the patronage of the Society for the Propagation of the Gospel."[54]

The following statements were taken from an article "Religious Patronage—Cyrene"[55] that was written by the director of the institution, the Rev. W. Ffrangcon Jones: "During the last 12 years of this school's existence art has exerted such a dominating influence that a very large number of former students are now recognizing what natural possibilities of expression for their practical knowledge painting and sculpture have to offer. In a unique way, instruction and training in art are proving to be a blessing for disabled persons. Although it is often torture for them to be dragged or brought here, sometimes for hundreds of miles, they still come, hoping against hope to be admitted. Here they have discovered latent talents which they never knew they had, and in some cases have found a way of supporting themselves in spite of the severest of handicaps.

"Except for those who are crippled, art plays a very minor role in the lowest classes, with only modeling taught in them. But beginning with form IV, attendance at art classes is obligatory for every pupil. The instruction and exercises take up two hours of every afternoon. In the beginning the pupils are supervised and observed closely; once their aptitudes for doing certain kinds of artwork have been determined, the gifted and promising pupils are put into groups which receive additional instruction, while the rest are trained for farm and carpenter work. Those who are crippled cannot perform manual labor and thus devote themselves entirely to the study and production of art. For this reason they very often display a greater proficiency than the pupils who are not physically impaired. One of the latter once sighed, 'I probably shall never become a good artist because I am not a cripple.'

"Cyrene is an island to itself as far as art is concerned. The forms of expression that were used by others in the past are vigorously ignored in the instructional program. This is done to counteract the student's temptation to copy slavishly, and also to stimulate him to come up with his own spontaneous style and develop it. It is interesting to compare the works of students coming from the various areas. Naturally the pictures of an urbanized African will be about trains, cars, and stores, while the students that have come from the rural areas choose themes from their tribal background. Both groups, however, soon begin to select themes from their new environment here in the Matopos district. Then, too, Bible stories they get to hear give them ideas for pictures. . . . And so the subject matter for the painter's brush comes from the Old and the New Testament, from the history of Africa, from folklore, and from the events of the day. . . .

"It stands to reason that art in Cyrene is still in its infancy. It is fostered chiefly through exhibits, through the interest and purchases of visitors, and also through occasional orders received from churches, government agencies, commercial firms, and architects. Murals were provided for the public buildings in Bulawayo, carved and painted bulletin boards were made for the mayor's official residence in Ndola, the altar in the Presbyterian church in Bulawayo was supplied with wood carving, and chairs were made for the clergy and the elders. Paintings were presented to the Archbishop of Canterbury and to Cuddesdon College in Oxford, and a carved cross, candle holders, and tables were made for the cathedral in Cape Town. The Central African Airways in Livingstone ordered some paintings. Besides these, various kinds of other orders were received, particularly also from parishes. The Museum of Natural History in New York and the County Art Gallery in Long Island, where successful exhibits had been held in 1955 and 1956, have works from Cyrene in their collections, and there have also been exhibits in England, West Germany, and South Africa that turned out well.

"I can find no better conclusion than a brief reference to two of our best artists. Samuel Songo is a Kalangan from Belingwe; both of his legs, his entire right side, and his right arm are disabled, in fact severely crippled. With his left hand needing all the support that his right can give it, he has painted and carved—yes, carved himself a niche in art that is worldwide. Lazarus Kumalo is a Tebelean from Essixvale; he too has been a cripple since childhood. His watercolors, like his sculptural works, have a bit of Assyrian tinge. His paintings are very exceptional and reveal a distinctive touch of their own in which cool bluish-gray colors predominate. Both artists are men of rare talents and accomplishments, both are a real credit to the school that offered them refuge and helped them on their way."

On the Way

The methods of doing mission work have changed completely, and a tremendous change has taken place in the position and status of the missionaries. The younger churches and *their* activity are now beginning to make their influence felt. Although the appearance of what we used to call "mission art" was a welcome sight then, today, however, it deserves a better name than ecumenical art. So far nothing has been said about the direction it should take. Whatever course it should happen to pursue, it will not take a person—not even one without an expert knowledge of art— very long to guess that it will not be like traveling on a superhighway at high speed and still being assured of a safe and smooth ride. Very much to the contrary! If anyone intends to get ahead on the road we have in mind, he must be prepared to do his best even on a bumpy road full of obstacles; he must face many problems, expect criticism, and again and again recognize afresh that he still is only an amateur and is in need of a great deal of experience from which he may learn. And that is not at all to be deplored. Indeed, it is good! Making desperate efforts to reach a goal that is rather clearly outlined in a person's mind and succeeding in doing so cannot help but be a rewarding experience.

Of course this cannot be accomplished, for instance, by merely wanting "to paint like the Japanese." We must bear in mind that the ancient art productions in Japan were without exception creations of Chinese and Korean artists and that before A. D. 1000 a truly Japanese art school was hard to find. But even after such schools came into being, "the Japanese style" was by no means the only style employed; indeed, from then on two separate styles were used and flourished side by side on Japanese soil: the old Chinese style and the Japanese style. Even to this day the old Chinese style is still being fostered with ever new modifications of the Chinese prototypes.[56] Thus the Christian artist in Japan must not only face the problem of selecting one of these two styles mentioned but must also worry still more about whether he has done the right thing after all in choosing only one of these styles and whether it is proper to limit the expression of Christian subject matter to these ancient alternatives, both now and in the days to come. The artist must also ask himself whether these ancient methods have not really become antiquated and whether it would not be in the best interest of art to join forces with today's modern production of art; if this were done, the author's personal opinion from this vantage point is that then the right things are sure to happen.

The African, too, has a similar problem. For the critics were wrong when they said that African art was dead or dying and that its revival would wind up in a historicism somewhat comparable to the revival of Gothic architecture in Europe. In this connection we have already quoted the remarks of Kevin Carrol; he and his carving school at Serima in Southern Rhodesia have demonstrated that this art is not dead but is in danger of dying from lack of orders.[57] African creators of art have absolutely no opportunity or intention of forsaking their ancient soil and starting over and accommodating themselves to new conditions, demands, and tasks. If it can be said, as it has been, that "until now we have barely begun to discover the styles or idioms through which the Christian soul of Asia and Africa can find its natural artistic voice,"[58] it is not to be construed only as a complaint; it involves far more: to say the very least, it is an indication of the stimulation art has received.

The moving about and constant searching that the artist feels compelled to do are determined by the peculiar nature of his work. This is true in Asia and Africa exactly as it is in Europe. For he wants to *say* something that will be "understood." He wants to be heard with the eyes! The Asiatics and Africans, who are right in the midst of today's turmoil, who are imbued with an intense nationalism, and who are opposed to every form of colonialism, though this new form might be only on a spiritual and cultural level, will not even pause to look at Western forms of art, especially not if they suspect this art is intended as a vehicle of communication. So art, too, in all its aspects and in the fullest sense, cannot be allowed to continue as the famous and often cited "flower-pot plant" that is imported from the West, whose roots are surrounded by European soil and prevented from making contact with the new soil by the solid surfaces of the flower pot. This kind of art cannot be fostered any longer, not even if one buries the whole works, pot and flower, in the ground, waters and tends it carefully, and it appears as if the flower had taken hold and were growing in the soil of India or Asia.

If we want to present the contents of the Bible to others in an effective oral manner, we must know in which age, in what place, and to which individuals we are speaking. In addition, we must take the greatest pains to learn the language of the country, not haphazardly but in a very systematic way so that we may be able to speak it fluently. In the same way it is quite self-evident that great care must be exercised in selecting the media and the forms of expression that are "current" in these countries in presenting the message of art on Biblical materials. Even art cannot speak a foreign language.

As we go along, we are trying to become better acquainted with the language of India's art, because we know that any artist painting in India does not and cannot claim that his brush speaks a representative and perfect language. In view of all this Johannes Beckman may have been correct to a certain extent—although it sounded strange at first—when he said that a distinctively Christian form of architecture or style of painting "had not yet appeared" in India.[59] This statement, however, must not be interpreted to mean that no progress has been made in the production of better art. Even Beckman speaks of first attempts that may have been widely rejected because they probably lacked a vigorous message. In my opinion "widely rejected" is not correct, and the reasons given for their rejection are just as false. Where there is art, there are also pros and cons, acceptance and rejection. The experience and impressions of the author, as well as the reviews in the literature, do not seem to justify such a universal condemnation, in fact they even contradict it "widely." And we may already have passed the stage of the very first attempts, as is indicated by the large number of entries in the exhibits, the good attendance, and the increased production. In the things that really matter, the objectives, Beckman seems to agree with us; like us, he insists *that* art must speak the native language of its respective country. And there's the rub. Even learning the language takes a good deal of time. And what has been learned must be practiced even though it means taking a chance that a slip of the tongue may occur now and then, that the beginner may make a bad impression, and that the still unpolished speaker or splutterer cannot make himself completely understood or that the language may not be the best and might be misunderstood.

The artists themselves hope that their command of the native language of art will improve from day to day, indeed the prospects are good that it will. Christians in the West share this hope with their colored brethren. (By the way, it should be remembered that "white" is a color, too!) It may be a good idea if we hear what some of the voices from this Western chorus have to say.

For instance, it was said "already" at the 1928 conference in Jerusalem that it is a sign of spiritual life in art and the acquisition of a native character when the worthwhile features of a country are accepted and used by it.[60]

Thirty years later at a conference of the International Missions Council in Ghana the same opinion was expressed in terser words. Although mindful of the risks involved, the group discussions emphatically declared that it would be highly desirable to see the Christian faith expressed in native forms. By not having to depend on European prototypes and having more appropriate means of expression available, the missionary can, in many cases, be of greater help than the older church leaders; for many of them found it impossible then to get rid of the ideas inculcated in their youth and could not oppose the missionaries who took a different view of the situation. It was in this connection that an African aptly said, "We want to be Africans, but not black Europeans!" And an Indonesian expressed his thoughts in this way, "We want to show that we (Christians), although considered nationalists and revolutionaries . . . are good Indonesians, too."[61]

In 1936 the apostolic delegate in the Belgian Congo, Msgr. Giovanni B. Dellepiane, issued this directive: "The Catholic Church is neither Belgian, neither French, neither English, neither Italian, neither American. But it is Belgian in Belgium, French in France, English in England, etc. In the Congo it must be Congolese. The lines, the colors, all elements of Congolese art must be taken into account in the erection of sanctuaries and in the production of liturgical appointments. So that when the Negroes are praying alone in the quiet church, when they are participating in the liturgical portions of the service, the whole edifice is praying and singing the praises of the Lord with them as a genuine expression of what their souls are experiencing. Then and then only has a church fulfilled its total mission among its people, both in the eyes of God and man. It is the Lord's house, it is God's house, and His presence fills it. It is the house of the faithful that has been built with their hands and decorated with their own art.

"If the church is the body of the eternal Christ, then in view of His incarnation and redemptive work the non-European cultures, too, are to be brought into the fold of the church with the same degree of love as the Greco-Roman culture once was; and thus Christian art, too, has an equal right to use Asiatic and African forms of expression as well as European. More is involved here than a concession to the heathen and newer Christians just for the sake of accommodating the missionary enterprise." According to Eph. 4:13, along with an understanding "of every human virtue, the culture and the art of all people also"[62] belong to the items that contribute to the mature manhood of a Christian. These words contain nothing essentially new, for similar statements have been made time and again from the days of Gregory the Great († 604) up to the time when the Congregation for the Propagation of the Faith published its directives for the first apostolic vicars in Eastern Asia (1659).[63] How long ago these words were said does not really matter. What does matter is that they be said over and over again! Nothing but good can come from hearing them expressed again in our day and in this way: "We are standing on the threshold of a new frontier in missionary activity that must concentrate on adaption and accomodation on a large scale. . . .[64] Thus in the not too distant future we can look for an African, a Chinese, and a Japanese form of the one holy Catholic faith, not only in its rituals but also in its ordinances, in its theology, and in its concepts of godliness. Then only can the church claim to be a true catholic church if it can allow for diversity and still maintain its unity."[65]

There is no reason why the Christians in India should want to exclude themselves from supporting the Hindu, Dr. Moti Chandra, who in speaking for art in India demands that the proponents of modern art should recognize the fact that Parisian and other forms of art, no matter how brilliant and progressive they might appear, are not really suitable for the artistic climate in India. And he does not forget to give the artists credit for keeping in mind that there are certain dangers

32

connected with slavish imitations and with constantly trying to develop their own forms and techniques in keeping with the genius of India. And he is also sure that in time a truly Indian style will gradually emerge from the initial chaos and from the senseless, technical experimenting, a style that is "international in its approach but welded to the soil."[66] These are also the very things that are emphasized by the Christians of India. In 1960 Christians and Hindus met to explore their common heritage; an announcement was made to the Hindus that the Indian church had now come of age and that "it is rooted in the soil of India."[67] Baptism does not cut the ground from under a person's feet. A. C. Chakraverti, who had been a very devout Hindu, inquired before his baptism and quite justly whether he could still be a true Indian after the baptismal act—he not only could but did and never became a brown European.[68] This is only one example among many others that are substantiated by experience and also by literature.

The productive artist from India, Angelo Da Fonseca, deplores the fact that Christians have depended on Europe far too long. His own determination is evident in word and deed: "I hope that we shall learn to treasure what belongs to our birthright and welcome it into our churches and homes."[69] No other artist in India has worked harder for this than he himself.

In Africa, too, we keep coming across the same determination. Today's Africans who have been freed from the shackles of colonialism like to speak of negritude, and in doing so stress that what they are really longing and searching for are the basic things involved in being a Negro and which must be maintained as a confession of the independent nature of their ancient African culture. These terms were first used by Senghor and the Afro-American author Aimé Césaire in the thirties.[70]

In this struggle the Christians are not only spectators. They are right in the thick of it. And we must not fail to notice that these strong roots of African nationalism are the result of the new ideas proclaimed by the missionaries and, in particular, of the emphasis they gave to the dignity of man. The missions have played no small part in supplying the driving force behind the movements for independence and have done so up to the time when the movements of the schismatic prophets were set in motion. These endeavors were labeled as a kind of "ecclesiastical instrument for radical nationalism."[71] No wonder then that Christians, too, are taking an interest in returning to African art, to music, dancing, and folk songs and are welcoming and endorsing a renaissance of things African. In 1959 at a conference in Accra the topic "Christianity and African Culture" was discussed. Here K. A. Busia as a Christian expressed in metaphorical language exactly the same ideas that form the burden of this book: "The African drinks from his own cup, a product of his cultural group, and not comparable with any other cup. All cups may be filled with water from the same well, but in spite of this they are not alike. Is it Christianity that imparts a different appearance to the cup, or is the water in the well a deciding factor here?"[72] What really matters here is that any kind of cup, whether it is an African cup or an Indian cup, may be used by all kinds of people to dip water from "God's little well that has plenty of water"—for all.[73]

How the obsession to use an African cup runs in the blood can be shown with only two examples. Italiaander tells of an African who was in Europe for the first time and with whom he went to the Folies Bergères in Paris. His young friend was fascinated by the dancing performance of the charming ballerinas. The following morning Italiaander asked him to paint a picture of what he had seen. He did—but all that could be seen was a group of Negroes dancing in front of jungle scenery. The European came to the conclusion, "He simply was not able 'to make the conversion.'"[74] Janheinz Jahn takes a different view of the matter, and in my opinion he is correct. "In reality, the African not only did the assignment but 'made the conversion' as well. He represented the event by capturing its meaning and transforming this meaning with his *own* determinators to convert it into a picture. And so this picture *evokes* dancing; its real intention was not to portray dancing. Italiaander wanted a picture, but the African produced a symbol."[75]

A few pages farther on in the same book Janheinz Jahn reports that the Ibibio Christians in southeastern Nigeria, in their drive to follow the modern trends, are forsaking their ancient practice as it is described by him and are erecting tombstones for their departed. These differ from their prototypes in that the dead are represented "colorfully according to their station" in life. "The men often wear European clothing, old-fashioned garments that make a person think of the dress of the early missionaries; the women are in African clothing with their hair in Ibibio coiffures. Some of the figures are reading a book, some are preaching, others are sitting in family circles, several are on horseback."[76] In this connection Hendrik Kraemer has come up with an interesting observation for Asia: he regards what happened as an Eastern invasion and characterizes it as "spiritually colonized by the Orient."[77]

In closing, I wish to call attention to something very special; I am referring to the deluxe edition of *Namban Art, Christian Art in Japan, 1549–1639*,[78] with which we have hardly become acquainted. It covers a span of 90 years and presents the earliest evidence in the form of 223 plates, 20 of which are in color, that then already Christian art in Japan was "on its way." The accompanying English booklet is a key that unlocks the work for him who does not know Japanese. The text describes the great persecution and how "the Christians in hiding" survived and then gives the titles of the paintings so that one can tell which pictures were painted by Japanese. Their subject matter will not be discussed any further here. The art of copying and the samples of transposed art are very interesting. For this reason the work also merits careful attention, especially by theologians, who hardly ever have an opportunity to learn of the severe persecution of the Christians in Japan and their perseverance although they were without churches and priests and forced to live in hiding. It is also valuable because it contains many illustrations of the so-called Pictures to Be Stepped On (Fumi-e) [print 218]. By stepping on this board, which often had carved figures on the upper side, Christians could symbolically—without saying a word!—renounce their faith in Christ and escape with their life by just taking this one "little step." The text and the pictures in Nishimura's work clearly show that already at that time an effort was made to catch the water of life in a "Japanese cup."

Criticism on the Way

Die Kunst der Jungen Kirchen was the first volume to outline for many of us the art activity of other countries which, until the appearance of the book, was practically unknown; even authorities on art felt the same way about the book. From the beginning knowledgeable men recognized that this work was a first attempt, even a daring attempt, and were delighted that an effort had been made to break virgin sod. They realized that someone had to begin and that in the beginning we never see the whole picture and surely not the finished and perfect product. When the book was declared to be "the best book yet on indigenous Christian art," and when announcements and reviews of it were kindly captioned "A book has become an event,"[79] even then questions were raised. Theologians must have suspected a specter of syncretism. In fact, in the future in articles involving syncretism all statements, not only those on art, will have to be examined for syncretism. That is a good idea. It is also quite in order to inquire whether and how far the theologians "should be allowed to venture forth into art history's thicket and its unavoidable temptation to *evaluate art*."[80] The author is a theologian.

The only new thing to be said here is that the author is preparing this work as a Christian and theologian. Now that the pictures have been assembled and made available, he hopes that interested persons will pay attention to them, view them with a critical eye, register their opinions for a later evaluation, and then regard these works, too, as a part of the whole field of art. It is true of course that this will require some empathy and familiarity with non-European ideas and art forms; this cannot be emphasized too often and too clearly. The verdict of a summary proceeding will not accomplish it. Many works might still be good art, even if they do not seem to elicit approval from purely European eyes and meet solely European standards. In the Holy Year 1950, as a German caught sight of a red-stained altar from Japan at an art exhibit in Rome, he exclaimed, "In front of such a thing I wouldn't be able to pray right." In this exclamation it is important to note the *I*, the I of the European—but would a Japanese have agreed with him? This causes us to wonder whether a Japanese would not have the same kind of reaction to a Gothic or a Baroque altar. In both the East and the West the traditional, familiar, and customary forms of art are always more appealing than the unfamiliar because they mean more to the inner life than meets the eye.

It hardly seems possible that even a group of European viewers could arrive at a unanimous verdict. As we have pointed out before, this should not surprise us at all. The same thing has happened to pure European art and to works that have come from the viewer's own country, and from a vicinity that is completely familiar to him, for where art is involved, there more or less understanding and acceptance is always found. How much more must this be the case when a different and new form of art is involved that for the time being must be more concerned about recognition than about approval and praise. If anyone feels inclined to offer criticism, he can be sure it will be accepted with thanks. We shall now give a summary of the criticism that has come to our attention.

1. One African reaction is surprising but understandable. Biblical illustrations were rejected because the portrayed persons had been given African features and an African appearance. And Africans objected to seeing Biblical figures portrayed as Africans. They declared that the pictures by Schnorr von Carolsfeld, Rudolf Schäfer, and other white artists had been very usable, that these paintings were meant to be understood and had also been well understood, and that they had found them helpful and good enough for them. A newsletter of the Stuttgart Bible Society says that pictures by Von Carolsfeld are in constant demand, that they are well received, and that they have even gotten into the Truck Testament that was printed a few years ago in the South Pacific. Through South Africa, Stuttgart learned that the Biblical illustrations of Von Carolsfeld appealed to the emotions of the people living there and they therefore liked them.[81]

A preference for old European pictures to which people have grown accustomed is also reported from other countries. However, this preference for European illustrations just may have more to it than mere tradition and lack of knowledge. This is shown by a very revealing reaction that occurred when Mark's illustrated Gospel first appeared in the Mende language and was becoming known. Dr. Eugene Nida reports concerning it:[82] "The illustrations in Mark's Gospel in the Mende language are acknowledged to be outstanding in many respects. Their design is simple; besides the persons there is little else that might distract the reader's attention or confuse him. The lines are sharp and clear, and the represented individuals are people that really look alive." The artist had thought he had done the right thing and had given the African brethren something in which they might take pleasure. But Dr. Nida feels constrained to go on: "However, a strange and unexpected reaction of the Mende people became apparent: they showed a conspicuous lack of interest in these pictures. They just did not like them."

Their reason is a total surprise, yet understandable if we take into consideration the existing conditions and the desire of the Africans to adopt today's modern ideas: the African Christians suspected that a new form of paternalism lay behind this edition! Even after a thorough self-examination, each of those responsible for this edition could have said that such a thought had never occurred to him. What then created this suspicion in the Mende folk? "Some of the Mende knew how people lived in the Middle East, and they felt that every attempt to portray people from the Middle East as Africans represented a kind of paternalism. The result was that this Gospel edition did not turn out to be as useful as people had thought and expected it would be," Dr. Nida wrote.

That is why those African Christians objected to seeing Biblical figures portrayed as if they were Africans. They felt that the European—and the American, too—wanted to speak to them in "a condescending way." This whole episode only goes to show that one, even with the best of intentions, can be misunderstood, and that a person must be very careful just when he "means well." We can be sure that a new (and so refined!) type of paternalism was the last thing that could have entered the minds of these men from the Bible Society, for it was rejected there exactly as it was in the circles of those who worked with and for the younger churches. William Fagg also tells about a similar attitude. He says that promoting appreciation of traditional African art was only an attempt to "hold back" the Africans in order to establish European domination even more firmly.[83]

It is apparent, too, that the Africans are not of one mind as to whether or not it is proper to use native art in the churches, especially for illustrating the Bible. This should not surprise us.

The same illustrations that aroused suspicion in the Mende people and were therefore rejected have, as Dr. Nida goes to on say, "been seen in other parts of Africa—and the people were thrilled beyond words at the prospect that the same kind of illustrations might be provided for their own edition of the Gospels." These two entirely opposite kinds of reception and criticism of the pictures show that we have just started to settle the questions concerning the problem of indigenous native art. This will still require much investigation, much work, and much patience. It is assumed that the reaction described may have originated with certain older men in key positions, men who had grown accustomed to European pictures earlier in life. In an effort to poll opinions on this matter it is a good idea to be impartial and not listen only to the "proven old men" who are in the limelight and who otherwise deserve respect, nor to the "loyal and deserving pastors and leading laymen." We should rather listen much more to the young church members, who are by far in the majority and represent the modern view and the future of the church.

2. Criticism of Alfred Thomas, who is from northern India, has also erupted, directed especially to the way Christ is represented.[84] The critics are not in the majority—as if the question of majority or minority were of any concern to admirers of his art! This is being said to dispel the mistaken notion that Thomas encountered only rejection or criticism or a large measure of it. The fact is that in general many have a great liking for his style of painting and find a message in his pictures. At least this is the case in Europe and in his native country. And we find the same kind of criticism, too, here at home and abroad—an indication that there still is no unanimity and indeed cannot be, as is usually the case! The things for which Thomas has been censured the Asiatics have expressed in one sentence: Everything smells and tastes too much like Buddhism or Hinduism. In Asia and likewise in Europe people feel that Thomas has gone too far in his endeavor to paint like the Indian artists. In his paintings Christ the Lord is represented as a Sadhu, with hair in Sadhu fashion and dressed in a penitential robe. Christ is portrayed as sitting like an Indian Guru in the lotus posture, that is, with legs crossed. He also has the typical gestures and holds His fingers in the symbolic position. That is really too Indic; it has already become Hinduistic or Buddhistic. In the opinion of a correspondent from Ceylon "Alfred Thomas is overstepping the bounds of what cannot possibly be considered permissible (as does Wajan Turun—this volume contains four pictures by him—in presenting a Balinesian Pedanda). With all due respect for the great artistic significance of his works, someone should tell him that his paintings unfortunately lack Christian insight."[85]

An artist from India wrote: "The paintings by Mr. A. Thomas are very good and have artistic merit. However, in my opinion they will not prove to be suitable for Christian purposes. This is the case because the artist has not told the true story of Jesus Christ and has not portrayed Him as true God, for his conception of Jesus Christ is that of Buddha. ... Should pictures like these ever find their way into the Bible or into any Christian literature, I would oppose their use humbly but firmly no matter who the artist might be. Understandably they would be a grave threat to Christianity. ... I declare emphatically that I am opposed to the idea of seeing Jesus represented as a Hindu holy man or as a Buddha or as a Buddhistic monk. ... If such pictures should get into Christian literature, the Hindus would think that Christianity is nothing else than another sect of Hinduism or of Buddhism. ... I sincerely hope that our historic background and our culture and the environment shaped by it will not get lost."[86] The reader may judge for himself by looking at the pictures of S.S. Bundellu in this volume how successful this critic has been in realizing his own ideal.

A theologian from India, Mark Karunakaran, has devoted two full columns to a discussion of the pictures by Alfred Thomas. He acknowledges that in every case the pictures dealing with the parables depict the truths the Gospels intended to convey. Nevertheless he, as a person who was a Hindu for 21 years of his life and thus is a first-generation Christian, can only see in these pictures endeavors that prompt him to ask: "Could they be misunderstood by Indic viewers? I would like to say they could not be! A Hindu would have no trouble at all in understanding them ... only he would not interpret them in a Christian sense." The critic fears that these pictures would open only another door for syncretism. He supports this contention with two examples of easily mistaken identity: Maríammal, the Hindu goddess, is confused with Maríammal, the Virgin Mary; and Krishna with Jesus. *Die Kunst der Jungen Kirchen* presents a picture of the temptation of Jesus (No. 14) in which, according to this theologian, "every Hindu would take the seated figure for the meditating Buddha." And in the picture of the stilling of the storm (No. 34) he sees a "picture of Rama." In both pictures he sees copies: the first is a "copy of Buddha pictures from the Ellora or Ajanta caves," the second is thought to be "copied from Ramayana."[88]

Four voices from the West shall also be heard. Bishop Stephen Neill, a man with long experience in India, welcomes every experiment that explores the kind of art familiar to the natives. But in this case it appears that Thomas has gone too far even for him: "In it our Lord looks like a young Hindu ascetic."[89] Apparently this Jesus also reminds him of Buddha. For right after the statement above he asks: "Is this kind of adaptation the wisest course to pursue? In my opinion a Buddhist would answer no. Buddha should always look exactly like Buddha." An American correspondent thinks that in picture No. 72, which shows the adulteress in the presence of Jesus, Jesus resembles a "floating Bodhisattva."[90] One of two art critics[91] is deeply disturbed "by the decorative manner in which the story of Christ's life and sufferings has been illustrated. It reminds us of an English variant of adolescent styling." The other has this observation: "Undoubtedly his (Alfred Thomas') paintings of the life of Jesus were designed down to the smallest detail to bring out as clearly as possible the Indian feeling and the familiar things connected with daily life in India, all of which bear the imprint of Hinduism and Buddhism. Then, too, it is amazing how skillfully the Gospel accounts can be translated into Indic forms of feeling, giving rise to creations so exquisitely beautiful and coloring so melodious and ingratiating that nothing else, even something more important, is able to prevail against their harmony and charm. Beauty and harmony are the things this artist was concerned about. For this reason his art is in danger of suffering the same fate that befell the English pre-Raphaelites and our German Nazarenes; their piety and sanctimony were emphasized too much and their far too peaceful and immaculate beauty became saccharine. This could happen to his art! And that is exactly what we believe we have overcome, in Europe at least, in favor of a new dependable authenticity which everyone in our day would welcome back. But it is quite possible that an Indian Christian does have the tender sense of feeling Thomas portrays. Here, then, is where the whole problem of judgment—and empathy— would show up. But why is it so completely different with Frank Wesley, Angelo Trindade, and Angelo Da Fonseca, for example, since they were likewise born in India?"

Also many of those who are delighted with the works of Thomas nevertheless find fault with them because on the whole they are too "sweet" and because Thomas' brush makes Jesus sometimes assume features entirely too feminine.

These criticisms have been presented in such detail because the pictures by Thomas were just the ones that sparked this criticism and because we are very interested in critical studies and discussions. We also hope to receive such criticisms.

Every person is entitled to his own subjective opinion. Why should an artist try to please everybody? Even Picasso does not do that in spite of his fame. If the artist has rendered a service, whether to a few or to many—be they Hindus or Christians, Asiatics or Europeans—he should be satisfied.

What happened to Thomas only serves to emphasize the short distance we have traveled on this way and how far away we still are from the goal. Of necessity, this way must be one that leads between Scylla and Charybdis. For a long time yet, if not forever, we and the Afro-Asiatic artists shall be in the same situation as the Basutho, Roy Moloi, who took the greatest of pains with his works in an endeavor to follow the "African way" and then wrote in January 1959: "When I first took up this style of painting, I often had to scratch my head in embarrassment." This embarrassed head scratching may very well be and remain a common sight in ecumenical affairs wherever the art of ecumenicity is in a stage of development. But above all, this will happen in all cases involving pictures of Jesus.

We may look at the picture of Christ with a critical eye. We may deplore the suggestion of an adolescent style and conclude that everything by Thomas is too sweet and too feminine. Most likely the artist would say in reply: My only "justification" is that *I* just happened to paint it that way—was I not entitled to be my real self? I painted this way at a certain stage in my development and career. Could I, the Thomas of that time, have done any different? No more than any painter could have worked in a style and manner foreign to him. I don't even want to be put on top; I am just one link in a chain of developments, a point on a long line. After my talks with him, I am quite positive that would have been his answer.

However, Thomas does not spell out and state his reasons that clearly. Therefore I will make an effort to shed some more light on one point in particular. On my two trips to England I looked him up several times in London and discussed many things with him, in his home and in his studio. It became quite evident that he had no intention of opening another door for syncretism or giving way to it. He was asked how he had arrived at this or that interpretation and representation, for instance, why he had portrayed the Tempter as a beautiful young woman, which had never been done before in the entire history of art (not even Botticelli).

His answer was typically Indic, and it is supported by many examples from literature. He said: I wanted to bring out the Tempter's wiles in a concentrated way, in a way that would portray their charming nature and seductive treachery. Since a woman is known to be the strongest seductive force, much stronger than even gold or power, I therefore gave the Evil Foe this form; I did so after much deliberation. In this connection we may remember that Luther, too, had said that the devil should not be portrayed in the worst way possible but rather in the likeness of a lost individual.[92] Alfred Thomas was informed of the published and oral criticism that his Christ looked like a Hindu or a Buddha to many viewers and that many believed he chose a woman to portray the Tempter because Buddha also was tempted by the daughters (plural!) of Maras, of which there are numerous representations. And many said that Thomas had known about them. Therefore it seems only reasonable to assume that this idea came from those pictures and must have crept into his brush unconsciously. Thomas immediately and emphatically stated that he had known nothing about these things and that this was the first time he had ever heard about them. This sounded creditable and logical. Christians of the second and third generation for the most part, we are ashamed to say, know precious little about the religions of their country and their own grandparents,[93] and also in many cases are firmly convinced "that there is *nothing* in the non-Christian religions that needs to be known." These words indicate that Mark Karuna-karan has no basis whatever for his suspicion expressed so positively that two paintings done by Thomas were copies. Nothing of the kind is the case, at any rate it did not take place consciously. Who is going to say and prove, or for that matter disprove, whether and how much the widely seen Buddha picture could have had an effect on the artist subconsciously?

Alfred Thomas showed many of his newer paintings to this author while visiting his studio. Among them was a *Judas*, which was also on display at the 1959 Edinburgh exhibit. This painting is indicative of the change in his style. What he wrote on February 26, 1959, is true: He has had enough of that controversial style of painting and is now assuming "as realistic" an attitude "as possible." He wants to portray "the naked truth," yet preserve the warm Oriental colorfulness and not let his paintings suffer from a lack of "Oriental touch." In those days he was compelled to occupy himself also with Old Testament materials because he had received some orders for them.

3. The severest criticism is fundamental in character.

A review had this to say: "In this case we cannot quite agree with the comments of the theologians from Halle, at least not where the setting for the manger in Bethlehem happens to be moved to an Indonesian jungle with brown-skinned Malayans worshiping the Child. The story must be preserved: Those who left their flocks and came with haste to the stable were Jews from the tribes of Judah and Benjamin. And our Lord was a Jew, as Luther has taken great pains to emphasize in his writings. The uniqueness of a respective mission field can be preserved only by things not historically related to it. Also in European art from the Middle Ages just those pieces are the most valuable to us from a theological point of view that have preserved the Semitic features of the disciples and other contemporaries of Jesus Christ during His earthly sojourn."[94] An artist from India has written to the author in a similar vein: He declares emphatically that Jesus was a man from Palestine and insists that He should be represented as such and nothing else, also in pictures. Just imagine for a moment, he went on to say, if someone would paint Abraham Lincoln looking like a man from India with turban and loincloth. It would never occur to anyone that this man is Abraham Lincoln. You would have to say first: "Warning, watch out! This man is Abraham Lincoln!" It is easy to understand what the writer of this letter was concerned about. And he has a right to be concerned. For this points directly to the problem that ought to be discussed with friends of painters and Christians of various countries—if they think there is any merit in discussing it with Europeans.

A voice from California seems to summarize the principal issues of this criticism: Really we should try to stay as close as possible to the actual situation in the Bible. Just because the writer of this letter has seen paintings that were "extremely Western" and others in which the apostles looked more like Germans or Englishmen than Semites, he is convinced: "It seems to me that the artist should always keep the Semitic situation in mind while painting. In the long run the message of the paintings would then have greater value and present a profounder truth."[95]

We who are just starting to become involved in this lengthy discussion to clear the air ought to pay careful attention to everything that is said, but especially to objections like those above. The fact is that at least one person gave serious sonsideration to what was said. This is demonstrated by the works of the American Negro artist Henry O. Tanner, who painted Biblical-Jewish types almost exclusively.[96]

Should we take one more step and give Christ "the features of mankind in general"? That has been tried in New Guinea, of all places, and without any influence from Europe whatever. When an altar in a newly erected church was in need of decorations, the matter was discussed and a definite conclusion reached that in no case whatever would a European design be considered.

The wood-carver commissioned to do the work withdrew himself completely for a long time. When he returned to society again, he brought with him a work of Papuan art that attracted attention for its uniqueness. The carver, Tine Kalai, had gotten a single sapling to grow into three crosses. The middle cross rose above both other crosses on which men "with an ordinary face" were hanging. The most remarkable feature of this work is the way in which Christ is represented: This Christ does not have either a brown Papuan or a white face. But He does bear the features of mankind in general, for no race or group of people can claim He belongs to them alone. This simple man had come to this conclusion and method of representation by reading the Bible. He had let the Jewish Christ become the "Savior of the world" (John 4:42), who indeed had been born in the land of the Jews but who nevertheless had come into the world to save all sinners and who in His Great Commission charged His disciples to go to all nations in the uttermost parts of the earth.

A Papuan artist has painted angels in a similar style, thus freeing them from the constraint of a set appearance.

Good enough! But what does an individual of mankind in general look like? Which features would the viewer give to this individual? Some artists, for instance Matisse in the chapel erected by him in Venice, have left the faces completely blank, leaving it up to the viewer to exercise the power of his imagination freely.[97]

But would not even the clothing alone compel the artist to commit himself? The paintings *The Good Shepherd* by Boschmann and *Christ and the Two Disciples* by Rouault were unusually well received in Japan. Such paintings were liked better than Japanese paintings for a quite surprising reason: That's international, that's the vogue in Japan today, and chances are that they will not be criticized but accepted.[98] There is little danger or hope that art will find a similar reception everywhere along the way toward its goal. To what extent this may apply to architecture, will be discussed later.

The more comments we seek to gather, the more evident it becomes to us that we are well on our way to a new start for brighter shores where we hope to find our long-range objectives. However, at this time they cannot be defined or described in detail. In the discussions along the way the pros and the cons are pitted against each other. Nobody is able to say, let alone decree, what Christian Afro-Asiatic art is to be like today or tomorrow. But what we can say is that there must be complete freedom in the production and judging of art. Having made this point clear, it must be admitted that most of the comments that have come to our attention advocate turning away in word and deed from everything Western, from every sort of influence by the last "Western colonies,"[99] and turning to a native art that has its roots in its own soil.

It may have become evident already, and it will become still more so in the course of this presentation, that the author is taking advantage of this declared freedom and using it to express his preference for and endorsement of native art. He is taking this position fully aware of the views, conclusions, and trends of thought that differ from his own. The broadmindedness so graciously ascribed to him[100] knows no bounds except this one: Everything that is converted or translated into other kinds of art and expressed in a new language of art must in every case agree with the old and eternal truth of Scripture. This means that nobody, also no artist, and nobody no matter how noble and mission-minded his intentions are, is to "take away" words from "this book."[101] In art, too, "Nothing can be added to it, nor anything taken from it."[102] Even if it is an African or an Asiatic cup, the contents must be the clear and pure water from God's well. If the full truth of Scripture is not violated and if the old and only saving Gospel becomes audible and understandable also through the unfamiliar voices of this art, then the apostle's words may find their full meaning here, in this other kind of proclamation when he says: "What does it matter...? In any case Christ will be preached."[103]

42

The Image of Christ

It is not our function nor is this the place to deal with the theological problems connected with the "image of God," nor to present the attitudes of the reformers and review the latest literature.[104]

Our chief concern, however, is closely related to all this. We are trying to introduce another image of Christ which did not originate in Italy or Holland, neither in Germany, nor America, within the range of observation and simply to say: *That* is here, too! When Karl Barth speaks of the "distressing episode of the image of Christ,"[105] it may be assumed from the beginning that also the Afro-Asiatic representations of Christ are a part of this very distressing story. For the artists and wood-carvers of other countries are faced with this same "unfortunate undertaking," with no brighter prospects and no greater resources than those of their Western colleagues, to whom Karl Barth has addressed himself particularly, if not exclusively.

If this characterization and the demand to desist from such efforts applies to European attempts, then they also must surely apply to all non-European attempts. If they do, then Rudolf Schäfer and Fritz von Uhde are in no better position than the non-German artists, for both groups are striving for the same thing. "The Offense of the Modern Representations of Christ" (these words are borrowed from the title of another article[106]) has showed up in the works of Alfred Thomas, as we have seen; and we shall continue to see offenses as long as art is produced and mistakes are made.

All artists do not share Karl Barth's views. One of these is Paul Althaus, who feels that Barth's objection together with its statement of arguments is presumptive and dogmatic in design; to him the history of the image of Christ "is actually not altogether 'distressing.'"[107] It will nevertheless be a distressing offense to many that Afro-Asiatic representations of Christ do not agree with the facts of history and real life in Palestine. We have said all along that this offense-provoking situation is with us. But we will have to bear this risk in mind and take our chances with offenses.

Painters and viewers alike must realize that representations can never really portray the complete image of Christ, and they must always recognize and understand that there is no basic solution to the "problem" of representing Jesus Christ as the God-man.[108] From the standpoint of the theological issues involved and the problems presented in communicating with a variety of people in the language of art "the Christian artist feels compelled" at one time or another "to hurl himself into this 'holy adventure' even though it could eventually mean his undoing."[109] The painter Emile Bernard once asked Paul Cézanne why he, too, did not paint a "Christ." He replied: "I would not even think of doing it for two reasons: First, because it has been done already, in fact better than one of us could do it, and, second, because it would be too difficult."[110] A person who says that deserves as much respect as he who tries it.

This venture, however, does first begin with conscious thought on the part of the artist in his workshop. It starts already, unintentionally and subconsciously, in the Bible reader who does not intentionally exclude any part or faculty of his total personality while reading the Holy Scriptures. No one has said it better or more simply than Luther, whose oft-quoted statement we can hardly avoid quoting here: "Of this I am certain, that God desires to have his works heard and read, especially the passion of our Lord. But it is impossible for me to hear and bear it in mind without forming mental images of it in my heart. For whether I will or not, when I hear of Christ, an image of a man hanging on a cross takes form in my heart, just as the reflection of my face naturally appears in the water when I look into it. If it is not a sin but good to have the image of Christ in my heart, why should it be a sin to have it in my eyes? This is especially true since the heart is more important than the eyes, and should be less stained by sin because it is the true abode and dwelling place of God."[111]

Where Christ is in the heart and set before a people's eyes, there it is "taken for granted," as Lothar Schreyer writes with commendable clarity, that in the minds of children from other races His image takes on the form and shape of their own respective race and people. This shows that Christ is not only the Savior and Redeemer of the Western world and the Caucasian race. He is the Savior of the whole world, who brings salvation to all people in every climate of the earth. This "taken for granted" has now become a reality: There is a yellow and a brown Christ, a red and a black Christ.

"Black and Beautiful Are You"

We shall now focus our attention on the black Christ, also on the black Madonna and the black angels. In this case it is quite proper for us to let the black Christ represent all others because this type has been discussed more thoroughly than any other and because through it, literally the darkest color, our concern for native art will be brought into clear and sharp focus. What will be said about this Christ may be applied also to every other color.

Above all, we must keep in mind that this set of problems, too, is embedded in dramatic events and experience, on a political and national level, and very closely connected with the problem of acculturation and assimilation, to which there still is not and never can be a clear-cut solution. It is said that today there is hardly an artist in Africa who works independently and that there are only a few left who have not succumbed to the influence of Europe. Rumor even has it that the African artists are apprentices of Europeanism and that some European artists today are closer to the African attitude toward art than many artists in Africa. At the same time the revival of pictorial art in Africa is still lagging far behind the writing and printing arts. Nevertheless, it is thought that a breakthrough has been detected in the creation of a new African art as has become evident in the works of the Afro-Cuban, Wifredo Lam, the initiator of a visual negritude.[113]

Efforts are being made in every area to preserve and promote the ancient traditional culture. Understandably, it will not be easy to extricate ourselves from this conflict between things African and European. "Recently I heard of an African girl who had not been admitted to a formal dance in Kumasi—by an African—because she was wearing our beautiful and attractive native costume instead of a formal. 'European dress only,' she was told."[114] This coincides with what has been heard from Cape Town in South Africa. In a stained-glass window St. Monica of Numidia is portrayed as a European woman in traditional Jewish dress, a most distressing sight. The curly Negro hair usually arranged in a wide variety of coiffures was used as one excuse for this action. Their radical dissimilarity was frightening and considered bizarre and ridiculous, as unworthy of sacred art. . . . Church decorum must be preserved.[115] A parallel situation is the expressed preference for black as a color and symbol. There black is not, as with us, the color of darkness, of something terrible and bad, of the evil, of death, and the realm of the dead.[116] "The whites insist the devil is black. When we blacks embrace a god, he must be a black one, and when we paint a devil, we paint him white, for the whites are the devils."[117]

In 1958 the film *Pilgrim's Progress* was shown in a school for African children. Naturally the question arose and was put to the poor teacher: "Why aren't there any black people in heaven? All the angels there were white."[118] The conclusion is obvious: "A Negro can never become an angel. Angels are white."[119]

During a Christmas program in British Guiana two angels were to appear. One angel was portrayed by a girl born in the East Indies and the other by a Negro girl. This was so unusual that the reaction, "But I have never seen a black angel before, they are always white," was almost to be expected.[120] These objections and expectations are found everywhere. Today the white color of angels is not merely a matter of color alone; for most Africans it is a constant source of provocation. In public relations and in the communicative process of church work the white forms act like barriers that as first impressions quite often then fix the path the hearer and viewer will follow. Of far greater significance as a repelling or drawing factor is the skin color of the Madonna. This is true in Protestant as well as in Catholic circles where, of course, the Madonna plays a far more important role because she is seen oftener.

It was quite typical therefore of the Japanese painter Fujita, who at the age of 75, together with his wife, was baptized in October 1958, to present the church of his baptism, the cathedral at Reims, with his first painting, *The Virgin and Her Child*.[121]

The Africans want to see the infant Jesus on "His black mother's breast."[122] On the other hand, where the whites had treated them with nothing but contempt and where their self-confidence has been shaken, if not destroyed, there might be "objection to a black Madonna. We are not used to seeing a black Madonna; she could prove to be less effective and less blessed than a white one. Years ago when the black Madonna from Katanga was shown in Jadotville, the typical protest characterized above was heard, 'We want the same Madonna as the whites have.'"[123]

Concerning this problem, too, the discussion veers back and forth, with a strange mixture of motives. Without a doubt the black Madonna has already won the battle. She creeps into the brush, the chisel, or the carver's knife as if it were the natural thing to do. And the Muntu face of Mary appears quite automatically.[124]

"Jesus was born of a white woman; we cannot follow Him"—a fateful conclusion, an obstacle that is sometimes almost insurmountable in our present situation.[125] We are concerned about "our color," and we are concerned about our coming into an African world. A poem expresses these thoughts in a touching way:

> "I'm looking for a painter
> to paint Madonna black like me—
> a virgin dressed in native costume
> as fine as mother's used to be.
> Listen, O sainted Mother:
> In the Orient you have a yellow face.
> The Indians think you're red
> as all their maidens are.
> And white folks say you're white
> as befits one full of grace:
> Then should you not be willing
> *to assume our color*, too?"
> "O Mother of God and of our Negro world,
> yes, tonight I'm coming
> to sing a song for you.
> O Mother of God and of our Negro world,
> black and beautiful are you."[126]

Professor Erkes of Leipzig saw a picture of the Madonna that was painted by a Chinese; in it she was dressed in Mandarin robes, had Mongolian features, and "a decidedly Chinese face," all portrayed from a Christian viewpoint. When this sinologue saw it, he praised "this fine quality of the Catholic missions, which is only one example among many others of the skillful manner in which they find a way into the inner mind of the Chinese people." He regarded this picture as "an ethnopsychologically, extraordinarily interesting item" of the Leipzig Museum of Ethnology.[127] Such an important voice is well qualified to arouse interest in the phenomenon of native Christian art among all people, also in regard to its ethnological significance.

This ethnopsychological interest will have to be concerned more than ever before with the black Christ, with the "Black Christ Dogma." There were black Christs already in the 16th and 17th century in the Congo and perhaps also in South Africa.

In Haiti, too, we come across the black Christ, as may be seen in the picture section. And of course the black Christ is no unfamiliar sight to the American Negro. Already in 1929 Countee Cullen gave one of his books the title *The Black Christ*. These lines are taken from a poem by him:

"... Ever at Thy glowing altar

Must my heart grow sick and falter

Wishing, He, I serve, were black.

Thinking then it would not lack

Precedent of pain to guide it

Let who would or might deride it;

Surely then this flesh would know

Yours had borne a kindred woe.

Lord, I fashion dark Gods, too,

Daring even to give to you

Dark, despairing features where

Crowned with dark rebellious hair,

Patience wavers just as much as

Mortal grief compels, while touches

Faint and slow, of anger, rise

To smitten cheek and weary eyes.

Lord, forgive me if my need

Sometimes shapes a human creed."[128]

The Negro spirituals say nothing about a black Christ.[129] From the time when this author first commented on the problem of a black Christ[130] the inclination to say nothing has become even more firmly entrenched. An African woman from Nigeria laments:

"Here we stand

infants overblown,

poised between two civilisations,

finding the balance irksome,

itching for something to happen,

to tip us one way or the other,

groping in the dark for a helping hand—

and finding none.

I'm tired, O my God, I'm tired,

I'm tired of hanging in the middle way—

But where can I go ?"[131]

It is a sad disappointment for Africans to find that they still do not have a picture of any kind of Christ helping a black person.[132] The people that said this evidently were thinking of a representation of the Good Samaritan. If they had said it about the Uganda people, it would not have been correct; most likely the Ugandans would have called their attention to a picture of Peter Paul Kasambe, in which the man that fell among the thieves is portrayed as a Negro.[133] But Africa is of gigantic size. Perhaps it would be a good idea sometime to summarize in one book everything that has ever been done there in the line of Christian art and make it available to all parts of that huge continent. Also the church periodicals should be glad to carry many of those African pictures. Many Africans would then see that more art of the kind they demand had already been produced than had been assumed.

On the one hand, some stress—occasionally with great fervor—the importance of representing Christ as a white person. On the other hand, this also happens: "In Cape Town, South Africa, Ronald Harrison, Negro artist, was haled before authorities because a painting of his shows Christ and Mary as colored people. Oh yes, two of the Roman centurions in the painting wear faces of Prime Minister Verwoerd and Minister of Justice Vorster."[134]

There is an extremely vocal insistence on a black Christ in the Separatist churches, where the aversion to everything Western is especially pronounced. There the foolish virgins have slyly become white and the wise virgins black. In a South African church there is a cross of dark bricks embedded in a white wall. In itself that does not appear to be anything unusual. But it did have a deeper significance! In the sermon the preacher asked whether anyone had ever seen a cross that was not white! He claimed the white man had perverted the cross and had made it a symbol of his white race. But God is a kind God, he said, and He is not a European! He insisted only a fool could say something like that. "Jesus has never set foot on European, American, or Australian soil. But Jesus has been in Africa!"[135]

Of course everybody knows very well that Jesus did not walk on this earth as an African or as a European. Occasionally it is also said that there are no black or white angels. There is an excellent solution to the race question, also in heaven: a transcendent, all-embracing color!

With an amusing twinkle in his eye the Zulu Makoba declared: "It is a plain and simple fact that Jesus tarried here on earth as a white person. When He returned to heaven, undoubtedly His skin took on a different color, Which? Certainly not any of those that are found among the people of South Africa. You see, if Jesus had kept His white color, He most surely would have erected a color bar in heaven, too. And then, even if I were ever such a nice fellow, I still could not get into heaven. If the skin color of Jesus were black in heaven, then of course it would be a pleasure for Him to erect a color bar against every color but black. But you seem to be a nice fellow, too. However, then you could not get into heaven either. Therefore I am convinced that all of us will have a different color in heaven, a transcendent color that is neither black nor white nor brown."[136]

But it must be said here that as far as we know no representations whatever of a black Christ demanded in other areas have come from the African sectarian groups that are permeated with a strong political feeling. The pictures of a black Christ included in this volume come frome those districts in which these sects are frowned upon or from regions in which this black Zionism is not represented. It would appear most natural for an African artist to paint from his own world of thought and then to transpose those ideas into this world. We also do the same thing. The European artists likewise have worked quite spontaneously, without asking for advice, without being afraid, and without offering an explanation; it was their own fiat that urged them on and still does. No one can paint in a more native style than Rudolf Schäfer did—equal rights for all!

It cannot be denied that in today's Africa and also in other countries nationalistic feeling is a contributing cause. But the clamor for native art that is rooted to the soil emanates also from such Christian considerations as the necessity for a personal spiritual life and a strong desire for genuine communication.

The underlying cause is deeply embedded.

The Final Reason

There is no doubt that the ultimate and real reason for the desire for native art and for bringing the Biblical events into the private world of experience and capacity for understanding is based on the incarnation. Ever since the incarnation of God and along with it, from the time of His entry into the visible world, a new dignity has been given the corporeally concrete things of this world. God has tabernacled *here*. God has assumed human form in a man of a definite nation: true God and true man. "The reality of God reveals itself in no other way than by placing me totally into world reality. But this world reality I always find borne, adapted, and reconciled by the reality of God."[137]

Through the incarnation God entered into the world of the bearer of His Word. God has spoken to us in our manner, as is evident from Holy Scripture's anthropomorphic way of speaking. One could use the everyday expression: God has accommodated Himself to man, to his receptivity, and to the limited capacity of human language.

It was a gracious condescension of God when He used human languages as the vehicle of His divine thoughts, that He also puts up with imperfect Bible translations and all manner of peculiarities in the sermons of the bearers of His message, and even accepts the witness of those who in a stammering and utterly inadequate manner retell the glad tidings. It is the one Gospel which in the diversity of languages and in manifold forms of thought and expression is carried into most varying circumstances and environments.

Grace cannot be generalized. There is no such thing as a spiritual-theological Esperanto. Grace does not destroy what we have; it completes nature. Thus art as a language by itself retains its originality. There is no uniform religious brush. The brush will remain Indian, Japanese, African. As in the case of spoken language, there is no language of art truly suitable for its exalted content. Nevertheless the condescension of God permits us to preach in pictures (Gal. 3:1) and to paint in our preaching: the Asiatic pastor and his artist colleague with all the speech forms available to them, the German village pastor or bishop with his colleagues in artist smocks in the manner transmitted to them, but differing from Asiatic art as it is understood in the West. All is yours— even the colors of the country!

Dr. Devanandan of India said in New Delhi in 1961: "This freedom is substantiated in the mystery of the incarnation. The Word was made flesh, the Son of God was made like His brethren. This is also the chief reason why we truly need indigenous churches and witnesses that speak and conduct themselves like the people whom they are addressing. For only in this way will the message of the Gospel become understandable and meaningful to the common man."[138]

Preaching is always and everywhere "translation," never pure communication, inasmuch as it is the communication of that which we could not know without revelation and preaching. It must ever be our foremost goal that by such "communication about" and "communication between" God and man and among men is eventually reestablished in the deeper levels of their spiritual being.[139]

Native art can be seen from the lofty viewpoint of communication. This insight is likewise expressed by the experienced and discerning authority, Dr. Eugene Nida,[140] who played an active and supportive role in the exhibit at Edinburgh in 1959.

Hendrik Kraemer also deserves mention here. He considered a truly native or a truly Indic Christianity as "badly needed," but it dare not be of dubious construction, an uncertain swaying to and fro, hence without the firm basis of the "Christian only."[141] Being truly Indic requires having Indic art forms also.

We may indeed see the specter of syncretism, but it is possible to oppose it, as Kraemer demanded. Syncretism signifies accommodation of content and eventuates in a synthesis of the contents of faith. Such syncretism is usually encountered more readily where the opinion exists that one can get along without communication conditioned by the indigenous.

"Indigenization" is nothing else than the necessary means for making relevant the good tidings of God within a group of people. In a great chapter on "Indigenization," to which we merely make reference for the benefit of the professional, A. C. Bouquet writes with reference to the frequently repeated charge that Christianity is a Western religion and the religion of the whites: "Nothing contributes more toward combating the misconception that the Christian faith is something foreign than the utilization of the painting and sculpture that is customary and familiar in a given country."[143] That is simply and correctly stated. Wherever this is done, and Bonquet also speaks of "very beautiful work" that has already been done, anyone who wants to become acquainted with the Christian faith need not begin with a prejudice and allow himself to be carried astray. Eddy Asirvatham of India has rightly and from personal experience called attention to this obstacle to communication.[144] It is our task to clear away obstacles and to hinder the construction of new barricades as far as it is in our power to do so. Shall we Christians do less than others and consciously permit the children of the world to be wiser than the children of light? In this context the observation is of interest that in Thailand in connection with the year 2500 of the Buddhist era a "Life of Buddha" was published "in Thai tradition" with pictures of Thai temples as well as classical paintings of Thailand art. The question was the restoration of works and copies by the painter Rudolf W. E. Hampe, born 1906 in Berlin, a resident of Thailand since 1933. A work of 184 pages with 65 colored pictures is a gift of the United States Information

Service to the Thailand people on the occasion of that great event and "in true Thai tradition and style."[145] A second life of Buddha with colored illustrations, which seem to have been painted in Burmese art, appeared in Manila.[146]

Our Christian concern in the matter can be very simply stated in Luther's Christmas hymn:

All praise to Thee, eternal God
Clothed in *our* garb of flesh and blood.[147]

There is no dearth of examples from experience to show with what gratitude this "our" is spoken and what spiritual meaning it can have if in the spoken and visual sermon the application, the *tua res agitur*, is made visible and thereby truly spoken *ad hominem*, if we may apply some current formulas from homiletics.

Wilhelm Oehler knew a Chinese who told him that as a student far from home he experienced some very trying hours. At that time it was a great comfort to him to have seen (seen!) the Savior on the cross and that he there was completely His and was understood by Him. At that time Jesus had the front part of His head shaved according to the Chinese custom of the time.[148]

An African missionary once passed along this story: One of his most faithful church members could never feel truly happy in his faith in Jesus. During the Sunday service he sat there quite troubled and with a sad mien, and the sermon did not help him along. But one day he looked different. The depression was gone, and he gave this reason for the change: Now I know it: Jesus was a black man.[149] At the same time he was well aware that Jesus was born a Jew, but had now ceased to be a stranger to him. Jesus had adopted his traits and had come very close to him. Thus He was truly recognized and accepted, for the African saw Him in his own flesh and blood.

A slightly condensed report on an African manger is given herewith. That Jesus was born in Bethlehem remained clear to all, yet He was brought into the tribal genus, into close intelligibleness, so that the viewers could exclaim: "He was born a Shambala!"[150]

"We modeled the clay figures in the size of about 8 to 12 inches. The head of Mary had become that of a Shambala maiden. She sat in the round hut in the light of a small oil lamp used by the natives. Her infant, however, was laid in her arms, for among her people the arm of the mother or grandmother is the cradle of the newborn, later on her back.

"In order to cover up the many defects of the figures as well as to liven up the gray tone, we clothed her in many-colored garments. A shawl was wrapped about our Mary's body. The second shawl hung loosely about the shoulders and partly covered the infant in her arms.

"Joseph received a long, light-brown shirt and was placed in front of the hut. A Shambala husband may take the newborn child into his arms only once and thereby acknowledge it as his own. After that he is not permitted to enter the hut during the first six weeks. He merely comes to the entrance of the hut every morning and evening to inquire about the condition of mother and child. He must also provide medicine and especially tonics for the mother: nuts, goat meat, and other needed things. He must also dress his wife anew with two varicolored cloths. For that reason the young father sits in front of the hut after the happy event and smokes 'the pipe of wisdom.'

"We had Joseph sitting and ready, but somehow something was missing from his figure. Then a little twig came into my hand which by its shape coaxed me to make it into a pipe. When Joseph received it into his hand and put it into his mouth, the teachers stopped from their work and looked my way in amazement and asked me to put the pipe away. 'No,' they said excitedly, 'leave Joseph as he is! Now he is a real Shambala, just as he must be.' All sorts of thoughts went through my mind: 'Yes, he must sit in that manner in front of the hut in Bethlehem to reflect on all of his duties as a father. How much more difficult they were here in a strange place and without adequate room! What a long pipe of wisdom he had to smoke now! And how many other things moved his heart from the time of God's first words up to the proclamation made by the shepherds!' So we let Joseph sit there as he was.

"And then the shepherds were formed. The first one received an expression of astonishment. A teacher unintentionally demonstrated it when I asked him about it. One hand is braced against his side, the other placed on his temple with the head bent forward. That is the manner in which the natives brace themselves when palpitation because of great astonishment comes upon them. . . . A shepherd's wife carrying a waterpot on her head likewise approaches the hut. Among the Shambala women water is the gift to a woman in childbed since she is not able to get the water herself because of the distance to the well.

"The celebration on Christmas Eve was over. Slowly the closely packed seats were emptied. Then the children gathered about our Christmas display and once again sang all their songs. When they finally left, I wanted to extinguish the candles. Then I saw the adults returning in small groups. Finally a Christian came with a pagan. One could recognize him by his face. It was only with difficulty that he could be dragged along. 'What are the Europeans with their stories to me, an old Shambala?'

"Suddenly his gaze turns into peering. His feet moved forward. What he sees before him is nothing strange! 'That is our living room, our people, our baby!' Bewildered astonishment spreads across his face. The news spread like wildfire: 'Jesus belongs to us! He has become a Shambala! He belongs to our people!'

"More and more groups, large and small, arrived during the next days 'to see this thing that has happened.' But they are not quite as attentive and quiet as on Christmas Eve. The joy is there. It does not only spread across the face as it does with us Europeans. On the contrary, the whole body of the African takes part in the rejoicing. This means that there is occasional shouting and jumping up and down. The church becomes Bethlehem, the place where the eternal God clothes Himself in our poor flesh and blood.

"The next year we again erected everything, but this time we did not construct a round hut but an open watchman's hut like those erected by our people in their fields. Thus the mother and her Child were easier to recognize.

"After the celebration a few greatly agitated women came to me and said: 'How could you do that to Mary and leave her in last year's dress! She must have new clothes like the rest of us when we have given birth to a child!'"

Poetry, Drama, Dancing, and Music

Each of these themes deserves treatment by itself. Unfortunately the materials are scattered about and difficult to trace, though they are available for use. For our purpose a resume of each would seem to suffice, including a reference to material already printed.[151] We need to be aware that something is being done in these areas, that we are not content to remain with the old but are striving for the new, and that something has been achieved. It is an indication of open-mindedness that the World Federation of Christian Students has likewise alerted its members to this field of endeavor and has devoted one issue of its publication to the theme "Faith, Art, and Culture." It relates that a conference was held in the Ecumenical Institute in Bossey, Switzerland, in April 1953, using the theme "Art and the Church"; likewise that a conference took place in 1954 in Holland, where the subject "Christian Faith and Drama" was discussed.[153] Such farsighted conferences were and still are necessary. It would not be difficult to furnish proof for the complaints heard in the younger churches bemoaning the fact that these churches are Western, even uttering the harsh judgment that they are "spiritual colonies of the West, copies of something, that they have not come of age"[154] or that they are "carbon copies of their parent bodies in America."[155]

The need has been disclosed and is undeniable, though it is possible that much has been written concerning it without appreciation of the initial difficulties.

Poetry

The church needs hymns for its services and for the home. For good reasons and in due appreciation of the hymnological heritage many hymns which have been taken over from the West and translated are still being sung, again and again. But there is also a treasure of hymns produced in the younger churches. Their number is so great that the book by G. Rosenkranz, *Das Lied der Kirche in der Welt* (The Hymns of the Church in the World), would need to be expanded. Their origin, frequently unexpected and spontaneous,[157] their musical form, and their theological content ought to be made the subject of thorough investigation. As far as the poetical aspect is concerned, little, sad to say, exists, and that solely on the part of the Roman Catholic Church. An Evangelical Tamil has written on "Christian Literature in the Tamil Language,"[158] but he was unable to name any present-day poets.

Along with European priests the Catholic quarterly *World Mission*[159] mentions two Indian teachers who were likewise authors. Both wrote in Hindi, Stephen Pundit authoring *Isuyana* (The Jesus Way), while Kerubim Barno Sahu produced *Mrityujayi* (The Victor over Death). In both cases the dates are missing.

Nothing has been mentioned in recent years of further poetical production on the part of Asiatic Christians in the literature available to this author. It was, however, reported and is to be accepted that the great *Christus-Purana* of the first Jesuit missionary, the Englishman Thomas Stephens, which appeared in Konkani, the native language of Goa, in Latin type and in four editions, was published in 1956 in Poona in the Marathi language. It is worthy of note that this translation was made by a Protestant who is also the editor, Prof. S. P. Bandelu, the chairman of the department of Marathi in the Protestant University College at Ahmednagar. Equally unselfish was the publisher, the Hindu Y. G. Yoshi, who produced this volume of 1,200 pages without regard for profit for only six rupees.

This *Purana* is a life of Jesus. It is divided into 95 songs of over 100 stanzas each in the form of an ode, in which three rhyming lines are concluded with a shorter fourth. Besides its clarity of Christian proclamation the volume is lauded for its "total makeup and decoration in true Hindu style" and for the "loveliness and musical cadence of the Marathi language"—and this by a university professor in a history of modern Marathi literature written by him.[160]

Even more welcome news comes from Africa, where the noteworthy contribution of an African of our time is deserving of appreciation. A report on it carries the heading *Ein schwarzer Heiland* (A Black Savior).[161] The poet, Dr. Alexis Kagame of Kabgayi in Ruanda, East Africa, son of a minor chieftain, born in 1912, and baptized at the age of 16, is a member of the first generation of priests of the infant church in Ruanda. It was his purpose to present the entire salvation history from the creation of the world to its blessed consummation in Hamite shepherd songs. The work, *The Divine Shepherd Epic*, is arranged in 150 songs. The author says concerning his literary aspirations: "I have no other ambition than to be a plain pioneer of Christian-African culture."

Drama

Religious drama is perhaps the equivalent of the German *Verkündigungsspiel* (proclamation play). The available material would be sufficient for an exhaustive treatment. This form of proclamation is being utilized by the church on its own initiative and in all parts of the world. Religious drama is very impressive and intelligible especially for ordinary people who cannot follow a sermon or a lecture in equal manner nor derive the same benefit from them.[162] It has proved itself to be one of the best means of communication. Eugene Nida tells of spontaneous presentations by South American Indians and arrives at the conclusion: "This type of spontaneous religious drama tells the viewer more than a long sermon could tell him."[163]

The play becomes the visible word capable of being experienced. In it bearing and gestures play an unusually important role and are often more expressive and effective than in the case of us Europeans.[164] The attention of students is also directed by the World Federation of Christian Students to the great importance of the drama as a medium of communication. They are asked to cooperate, but are also given a plain warning and exhorted to self-criticism; they must not use drama as a hobbyhorse and must guard against amateurish presentations.[165]

In the Indian world, to which the drama is familar,[166] Christians also have cultivated this heritage. Already at the time of Robert de Nobilis "sacred plays" and "mystery plays" were presented in South India and Ceylon.[167] In the century before him it is reported: "The truths of the Christian faith were brought home to college students and believers and impressed effectively upon their memory also by means of theater plays and so-called dialogs. Thus in 1568 in a college at Cochin a "dialog" between Abraham and Isaac took place; likewise the parable of the rich man and poor Lazarus. In Goa the imprisonment of the apostle Paul was dramatized in 1571, the story of the prodigal son in 1575 "with much stage equipment," and the coronation of King Solomon in 1578. Finally, mention should be made of the 16th-century presentation of "Balaam and Jehoshaphat," which took place in 1579 in Goa and definitely directed the attention of the audience to the conversion of the heathen.[168]

The misgiving about women acting and singing is still under discussion. Many Christians are progressive in this respect and discard the ancient custom. Thus in a suburb of Colombo (Ceylon, now again Lanka) Christian women publicly put on a play for the laity.[169] Fellow patients are entertained by means of plays.[170]

To acquaint the nearly 300 students from kindergarten to college with the great world religions, *A Passion Play in Ahmedabad* was given by Hindus. The play embraced the entire life of Jesus. "When the performance ended, some of the viewers, moved with emotion, burst into tears and touched the feet of the actor who represented Jesus." "When Christ appeared, it was as if He had cast a spell over the entire environment with His priestly gestures." The report in the widely circulated *Illustrated Weekly of India* carried six color pictures.[171]

The Indian, P. Solomon, "also saw a play in which Jesus appeared, and everything was done with respect and devotion so that no one could find fault with it." At present two people are devoting most of their time to religious drama, namely, Rev. Darius L. Swann and Miss Joyce M. Peel. Their report on the "Indian Oberammergau" as well as the following statements are most welcome and noteworthy: There are "drama schools" today in Dehra Dun and Mussooree in North India and in Bangalore and Madras in South India. In the summer of 1961 a workshop was conducted in Mussooree for men of literary talent, of whom one could expect cooperation in a project which was begun immediately. A course was also given in which authors and potential writers, poets, musicians, and dancers were brought together. One result was a dance drama on the life of Moses, which was presented in St. Thomas Girls' High School in New Delhi. The lines were done in "the finest Hindi," and the music is no other than classical music, composed and sung by artists of All India Radio. Even the dance steps were arranged by professional dancers in order to exclude everything of an amateurish nature and to maintain the proper standards.

In Allahabad a Christian dramatic society named Galili Natya Sangh was organized, whose membership mostly attend the university. The English language as well as English works are used there. Henri Ghéon's *The Mystery of the Finding of the Cross* enjoyed such success that its presentation was desired in many other cities. The people at that place not only mean well but render it so well that it may rightly be said to have already achieved an almost professional standard expected of professional players.

The liturgical drama is likewise cultivated. Such a service was held in New Delhi with the theme "Christ, the Light of the World" when the Ecumenical Council convened there in 1961. "Now that is real worship after our fashion," said an Indian who was first compelled to overcome a critical attitude toward such presentations. Various performances, some of them dealing with psalms, have now been able to do away with various misgivings. The epic drama *From Abraham to Nehemiah*, done in Tamil and containing much Old Testament material, has been called the greatest project ever undertaken. A film version of it has been prepared by the Mass Communication Department in Jabalpur.[172]

Reports on a Christian dance drama presented on Catholic Day in Munich in 1960 bearing the title *The Fruit of Death and the Bread of Life* have circulated in the press. The dance group had come from Bombay. "This magnificent success surpassed all expectations. The colored representatives from all parts of the world experienced the greatest excitement and did not hold back with their approval." Everything in this dance drama was Old Indian: the Sanskrit of the text, the music and the songs in Hindustani ragas, the dancing technique according to the classical dancing style of Kathakali and Bharata Natyam. Such was the praise the Indian cardinal, Archbishop Gracias of Bombay, heaped on the performance.[173]

Also among Tibetans living pictures in which free playing and solemn dignity, the gruesome and the poetic alternate, and which contain dialogs of great beauty have been very impressive at Christmas and Easter time. The advisability of sending a small group from village to village to proclaim the Gospel in this manner is being considered.[174]

Similar reports are coming from Malaya and Thailand. The Christmas story was presented in a leper colony. The silent scene depicting Joseph and Mary seeking shelter was especially impressive when nothing but silently refusing hands were to be seen. Even King Herod appeared at the manger and shouted out into the church: "I will not have this man to rule over me!" As a gift Herod laid down before the crib—his sword for the murder of the innocents. The leaders of Israel likewise brought their gifts to the manger. They dragged in a large cross, erected it, and screamed in unison, "Crucify Him, crucify Him!"

A few years ago the resurrection of Jesus was presented in Tokyo, Japan, in the strict form of the ancient Japanese *noh* dance drama. Two pictures shown in the report give an insight into the genuineness of everything, also of the clothing and music. It is said that it belongs to the essence of *noh* to consume 20 minutes in playing what could be said as well in two. Thus 50 minutes were required in reproducing a 2-page text. The reporter stated: "For the first time the drum is beaten when Christ gets ready to execute the great dance in a resplendent, divine robe: indescribably light, floating, yet standing firmly on the ground, divine and totally human at the same time... Idol-play had become God-play. The text followed the Holy Scriptures with all strictness. ... The world of *noh*, in which the play took place, had not been touched in its beauty and autonomy, but this world had become new and bright in Christian Easter exultation."[176]

Drama and dance belong together. Therefore mention must also be made of the dance drama *Dance of Mary Magdalene,* which elicited high praise from the many spectators who attended the anniversary celebration of the Evangelical Mission in Japan in November 1959. Everything was done in genuine Japanese style, and everything was a genuine proclamation of the Gospel. It was a doxology of divine grace! The form corresponded to the content, for perhaps "there is no other dance which in its chasteness is so suited for a religious theme as the Japanese dance." All the dancers were Christians. The leader of the group had at one time been very ill and overheard the remark of her doctor to her loved ones that there was no hope of recovery. This had driven her into fervent prayer to Him with whom nothing is impossible. She recovered and vowed to place her gifts as a dancer into the service of God. In reading the program with its remarks about the music and the songs, one can readily understand that this very large audience was spellbound, edified, and blessed, and it could justly be called a deep experience."[177]

Africa, too, has its plays of the most diverse kinds, manger plays being special favorites.[178] In Matabeleland (Rhodesia) the 14 stations of the cross were portrayed by African Christians, photographed in color, and displayed in some churches in lieu of genuine works of art. This first attempt was a genuine "black Way of the Cross," and as such it will doubtless be preferred in every case to European works even when the latter would be given recognition as superior works of art. The portrayal of the sixth station makes a winning and persuasive impression.[179] A wide English and German readership was able to gain an impression of the nature of this mode of presentation and proclamation by means of the publication *Afrikanische Passion* (African Passion). The introduction by John V. Taylor and the 24 prints have dispelled many scrupels and silenced premature criticism.[180]

In the Catholic mission an additional step was taken. In Gwelo of Southern Rhodesia the erection of an amphitheater has paved the way for Africans who possess talent for acting and intend to develop and use them.[181]

From New Guinea, rich in presentations of this type, we shall adduce but one example from the abundance available. Nurses, attendants, and patients of a Lutheran hospital presented the Christmas story in the church. A colorful scene showed brown Mary and in her lap the Child that had been born the week before. All strangeness had disappeared; a genuine realization had been gained. People understood that this Jesus came also for us and to us."[182]

The Dance

The question whether and to what extent the church should (again) accept and even promote dancing on the part of the African Christians has not been decided unanimously[183]—as was to be expected—nor is such a decision likely. A firm rejection of it was encountered not only among the missionaries but among the African Christians as well. Furthermore, no church regulations have as yet been established.[184] On the whole, however, a change has occurred which places the dance and its cultivation into a far different light. The faculty of Concordia Seminary in St. Louis, Mo., has accepted a master's thesis on the dance in the younger churches.[185] This successful thesis surveys the entire area and offers a helpful bibliography and much positive material without, however, ignoring the critical and suspicious voices.

It is in poor taste to raise accusations against the older missionaries and to ridicule their narrow-mindedness, which logically led them to hold that there was no room for rhythm, movement, and color in the worship services and that a Europeanized African church needed renewal at precisely this point.[186] We today know much more about the nature of "primitive" man as well as his dances and understand that the older generation did not merely misjudge by appearances and was not wrong in every case when in many instances it characterized the dances as obscene and emphasized their religious relationships. Yet credit is due Catholic missionaries who after many decades arrived at a better understanding of the "false assessment of the native psyche in the South Sea missions" and candidly report how this took place and how they came to a totally different understanding of the sexual emphasis in night dances: "Accordingly, it is not cheap eroticism that is being offered here, but the very opposite. By presenting the impious tempters in person, one gains power over them and is able to restrain their pernicious practices and give earnest warning to the young. By misunderstanding the native mentality we are also prone to condemn things as immoral which, if viewed also from the viewpoint of the already Christianized natives, can be fully justified."[187] "We know that dancing, 'the poetry of movement,' is part of the African's idea of being totally human. ... When my wife died, my father-in-law came and told me to dance. And I danced in deep sorrow."[188] In most cases access into this world remains closed to the whites, also to the Negro who happens to live in the United States. Richard Wright has written about dances which he saw on African soil when a death had occurred. He, an American Negro, concludes his detailed description with the informative words which excuse not a few white missionaries even now: "I understood nothing. I was black, and they were black, but my black skin gave me no help."[189]

Today we well know that "primitive religion was danced out rather than thought out."[190] Such dances are different and more than a pleasant pastime or erotic attraction, especially in view of the fact that men do not dance with women. The dance is at once a manifestation of life and vitality and a religious act.[191] Unlike the pioneer missionaries, we are today dealing with the second and third generation of Christians; the Christian proclamation has had a leavening effect in not a few places. It is now no longer said at a war dance: "We have strung up their entrails all over the place."[192] This change can best be seen by noting that at such a representative gathering as the first Pan-African Christian Conference in Nigeria (1958) the efforts seeking to combine the African cult dance as an original element of worship with the forms of Christian worship was welcomed.[193] Also dance customs needed to be baptized!

At this point we can only quote a few illustrative references from the many reports on the new attitude toward the dance and its acceptance into the life of the church. To begin with, an example from the Arctic region: "A sliding door separates the chapel from my large living room, and a few of the natives (Eskimos) had asked me whether they would be permitted to use it for a dance on Christmas Eve. ... The crowd began to arrive at about 8 o'clock. All of the natives had donned their best clothes. ... It was a memorable dance. ... About midnight, as I began my preparations for the Mass, Ed turned off the music and announced that the dance had ended. We closed the door between both rooms. In a happy mood the dancers went out-of-doors to cool off a bit before the service. Only a handful of the natives in the camp were Catholics, but almost all the families crowded into the mission when I rang the church bell."[194]

In order to abolish the ancient dance songs among the Kanakas in the South Sea Islands, native poets and composers were invited to create new songs, and prizes were offered. The result? "On holidays dances of religious contents were frequently held, for instance, the Passion of Christ and the 14 stations of the cross, concluding with our Savior's resurrection, etc. At other occasions the dead of the clan are honored or happy scenes are enjoyed which frequently are in the nature of people's courts.[195]

New Guinea is regarded as the land with the greatest variety of religious dances. Also Christians dance a great deal, but they dance their own dances. Thus at baptisms they dance with palm branches in their hands, accompanied by the roll of drums at the head of the baptismal procession, as David of old danced before the ark of the covenant. They also dance Bible verses, among them the words about "the wiles of the devil." There is no celebration without a dance. Also the peace dance is represented."[196]

A collection of poems by an Indian poet contains also a song for the classical dance "Bharata Natyam." The singer thanks the Lord for this sublime art, for the suppleness of his limbs, and for gracefulness in holding the fingers, singing, "Thine is the orchestra," etc. The classical Indian dance is taught also in many Christian schools.[197]

Thomas Ohm, a student of missions, specifically calls attention to the possibilities offered in the dance and in play and as a man of theory as well as an expert in practice welcomes anything that is done in these areas.[198] Mention might be made of the dance group from Bombay.

Along with Catholic Christians the question is also being asked by Evangelicals why "dancing before the Lord should be neglected." Also the latter definitely desire that dancing compositions be promoted as an expression of Christian thought and an interpretation of Christianity's historical events. Already a revival of dancing is being discerned and the wish expressed that the dance be incorporated into the life of the church for the interpretation of Christian themes. The dance, like music, must be "baptized into Christ." People are asking quite urgently: "What has the Indian church done about the ancient art of dancing, this glorious diamond jewel? If it is baptized, it can serve to the praise of our Lord."[199]

Why do congregations arrange a joyful dance after the Communion service? The European asks how that agrees with Holy Communion. The answer is: "Shall we not rejoice over the forgiveness of our sins?"[200]

When Orthodox theologians visited the Thomas Christians in South India after the convention at New Delhi in 1961, they had the experience of witnessing how dancers accompanied the processional cross and the orchestra in the processions and how at the reception and the evening meal everything was in the framework of Indian folk songs as well as dances.[201]

And Africa![202]

Henry Weman begins the chapter on the sacral dance with the statement: "Without a doubt the right position toward the dance (in Africa) presents a difficult problem. But if it is true that it is impossible 'to forbid African drum-beating and dancing without confusing and disturbing the life of the soul,' this alone ought to suffice to make this activity an object of thorough rethinking."[203] What is here said about the Evangelical churches holds true also of the Catholic churches. A modern church plan even provides an oval area for dancing. This is the most typical and farthest-reaching expression of the new open-mindedness which allows African Christians to remain truly and completely African.[204]

Dancing is a typical mark of the Messianic sects. There are some repulsive features connected with it, but we mention them here[205] because misuse and mistakes must be reckoned with everywhere. We are at this point interested particularly in the Christians of the churches, who dance at the installation of their bishop. There is dancing in the church service of the Cameroons and after the pronouncement of the forgiveness of sins,[206] the offering plates are carried in dancing fashion, and gifts are brought forward and made in the same manner; the choir enters "singing and rhythmically swinging their bodies."[207] In some African churches "dancing is a part of the Communion service." "Joy was just about considered the outward sign of revival. It was not only reflected in their faces, but in true African style expressed itself in song and dance. Frequently dancing and singing took place in front of the church after the services."[208] An Anglican regrets that "something as English as our Common Prayerbook (with its appeal to frost and snow to praise the Lord!) is to remain in use in Ghana without change. He had elders lead the singing—this was out-of-doors—and the entire congregation sang the chorus to rhythmic dancing. "I can tell you there was swing to it." And the "dullness of decorum" was dispelled in favor of the African.[209]

Dancing on the part of Christians both in and outside the church has deep human and spiritual significance. There is more involved than the idea we get when the word "dance" is mentioned. We can take it from an experienced man that "so long as the African cannot sing and dance in Christ, the average Christian will not penetrate into the deeper meaning of faith in Christ." He desires that the separation of faith and art and the subsequent introversion of church life and the neglect of the rituals that are so essential for the African should once and for all be abolished. He also demands in addition the cultivation of dancing in the wake of a needed reinterpretation of the world of symbols.[210] A Catholic voiced the same sentiment: "I cannot imagine how Africans can praise God without dancing, since that is such an important part of their world." This reminds us of a film on the first National Eucharistic Congress on the Gold Coast in 1951: "There one could see their dancing in the final procession."[211]

At the Second Pan-African Lutheran Conference in Antsirabe (Madagascar) in 1960 the Christians began to dance "without inhibitions during the spiritual songs, a beautiful, persuasive proof of how joy moves body and soul to a single praise of God."[212]

Witness is part of our spiritual existence, and the dance drama is eminently suited for precisely this because it brings home to the spectator, let us say, the story of David, of the prodigal son, or of Isaac and Rebekah as well as Christmas and Passion plays in a vivid manner and without foreign elements, as befits their art.[213]

This art is also emphasized by an observation of Richard Wright which deserves to be noted. He writes: "I stepped out onto the balcony and saw the Prime Minister (Dr. Nkrumah) dancing by himself on the lawn."[214]

Music

At this point we want to indicate the state of affairs in the new aspirations of native music and its cultivation. Among major works we shall mention only Henry Weman's study[215] and a dissertation by a Ghanian on West-African music and its use in ecclesiastical life, the dissertation of Fr. Stephen B.G. Mbunga, "Church Law and Bantu Music" (1963), and the volume: *IV. International Congress for Church Music in Cologne, June 22—30, 1962.* Numerous magazine articles also report on various aspects and geographical areas.

Not artistic church music but the congregational hymn is the most important. Statistics would presumably demonstrate that the Western hymn and the Western melody still predominate. Whosoever would cast stones at the pioneer missionary should be asked how he, if he had been in their place, would have wished to arrive at the knowledge and use of native music and suitable melodies, not to mention the texts. We cannot produce in sufficient number hymns suited to a particular nation, nor can we have them produced. They must flow forth from the younger congregations if we are to have them.

Nevertheless, the European melodies should not be discarded root and branch. It is too late for that, even if it should appear desirable. Many of them have found their way into the hearts of the young Christians. Also Western music will remain. Even the works of Handel and Bach are sung very well in many places, also in the South Sea Islands. Western music is of abiding value as an ecumenical bridge. Daughter churches may accept an inheritance from their mother churches.

The normal thing is and will continue to be that Christians feel at home when they sing and make music. "It has a Western flavor" is no longer a recommendation to outsiders.[216] The words and melodies frequently suffer violence in translation. And hymns and liturgical pieces that are squeezed into foreign language and music forms may sound very unpleasant, as a South Indian bishop assures us, who is then reminded of a famous statement in a different context: "It is like a dog walking on his hind legs—it isn't done well, but one is surprised that it is done at all."[217] The story of a taxi driver in India drives the same point home with equal emphasis. Asked when the service in a certain church would conclude, he answered: "I do not know; there is always some loud noise there at least four times. Until now I have heard only two."[218]

Also where European melodies are appreciated and people have become accustomed to them and sing them well, the singing lags far behind the native. That is due to the melodies and their foreign origin, and most certainly also to the way people have learned to sing them. Two experienced men rightly say of Mexico and Africa that the singing in the churches is frequently a "boring and tiresome dragging along," "difficult and slow" in its effect, while the singing of the African sects is much livelier and more joyful.[219] From our own and frequently depressing experiences in our church we learn to understand such complaints. How seldom the singing of a German congregation exerts a winning influence! It is a fact and for creative artists a cause for complaint that the church does more for music than for creative art. It is said of Rome that never before has it issued so many directives for religious architecture, sculpture, painting, and other forms of art. To be sure, it was done, but never so often and with such urgency and precise details as it was done with regard to church music and singing.[220] Nevertheless, much more has been accomplished with the little complained about by the Catholics than has been accomplished by the Evangelicals. Among the latter, who is concerned about singing and music in the younger churches and willing to supply funds for it? How easy it would be to stir up interest and helpful activities among the many choirs and church musicians in Europe and America, especially in the name of the current and almost magic term "ecumenicity"!

Roman Catholic Christians have a "Catechism in Songs" in verse and in classical Hindustani ragas; likewise psalms in the same musical form.[221] The composer is Father Edmond, who studied Indian music for nine years and earned three academic degress. Since 1956 he has been superintendent of the Summer School of Hindustani Music (S.S.H.M.) in the Naini valley district. The school requires hard work and has a demanding final examination. The enrollment in 1956—1960 was about 400 priests, brothers, nuns, laymen, and women. Every year the number increased. By way of comparison what are the few students who receive scholarships to study music in Europe?

It may be presumed and is to be hoped that much goes on which receives no publicity.

It is all the more refreshing, however, to be able to read about the introduction and use of native instruments or even of an African cantata;[222] or also of a "native folk Mass" which is not accompanied by an organ (or a harmonium) but by a drum, or of a choir in Cameroon which has replaced the former singing with African singing accompanied by a drum, hand-clapping, and the customary horns.[223] Welcome news came from Sumatra, where the use of the "animated music of the Gondang," a kind of metal drum, had been forbidden, which is doubtless to be traced back to Missionary Ludwig Nommensen. The prohibition, which had been in force for about a generation, was lifted in 1938. "Thus the ancient heritage, which had more or less lost its animistic content, made its reappearance as a 'cultural contribution' of the Batak community."[224]

With special gratitude we take note of a Pan-Japanese church music convention that took place Oct. 9—11, 1959, in Hiroshima. It was the first convention of its kind, arranged jointly by Protestant, Orthodox, and Catholic churches. Once again it is significant that not a word was to be found on it in the Evangelical press, but only in a Catholic publication.[225] Among the various new presentations offered there a Passion Oratorium made the strongest impression on the Japanese. The Japanese Franciscan P.T.M. Sueyoshi stated that in his research for his dissertation he had accidentally come upon a report on 40 to 50 mystery plays that had been given in the early mission church of Japan with Japanese instruments in Yamaguchi and Kyushu with great success and had always attracted large crowds. Thus Japanese Christians already at that time brought their gifts to the manger.

"The mournful song" in most churches—and the Catholic Christians prefer Protestant hymnody to that of their own—must give way to another, a better one, it is claimed.

When a psalm was rendered by a choir at this meeting, without revealing its origin, there was enthusiastic applause—and a Japanese remarked to his neighbor: "Wonderful French thematics." He would have been a philosopher had he kept still, for the melody was borrowed from a folk song that is still being sung on the Japanese island of Sado. Some uncertainty became apparent when the use of a Japanese guitar, the samisen, was discussed. One group said: "Samisens remind us of sake wine, of geishas, and of noise." Others thought: "It does not appeal to the better nature of people." Still others favored it. This example shows what is valid for the entire area of ecumenical art: Much is still in the process of becoming; we are only, but already, under way; much time will still have to be spent in reflection and discussion. The final and true decision lies with the children of those countries.

In Hiroshima the Catholics support their own music academy. The Protestants have none, neither in Japan nor anywhere else.

Architecture

Discussion of professional insights and reflections concerning the principles of past and present-day church construction is not the task of the author. We are merely calling attention to previous surveys of church building in the younger churches.[226] It is an almost superfluous observation that also in the erection of churches in Africa and Asia function determines the forms of building and that the specific theological consideration and the liturgical, in fact the worship life of the congregation, must always be and remain in the starting point.

The entire area of overseas church construction is still in need of serious and, in part, initial fundamental preparation. We suggest that the World Council of Churches include in its manifold study the question of church construction outside Europe and bring together architects and theologians for that purpose. The often-discussed lay activity could thus be actualized and a question of genuine ecclesiastical and ecumenical significance be tackled.

This volume concerns itself solely with modest references to questions and preliminary solutions already existing. Attention is directed to an important field of endeavor and the invitation to cooperate extended to professional men in order that the evident, the outward and visible form of the church, might achieve the most suitable form. Yet this dare never be a static solution. Every supposedly final solution would be sure to remain sterile, because the true solution cannot be given in the form of a theory but only in the creative multiplicity of art, which is ever in the process of becoming new. This will require much experimenting by sharp heads and pious hearts, constant searching and groping about in Christian patience. There is but little special literature on this subject, at least to the knowledge of this writer, likewise no monographic dissertation in any part of the world, for their existence would surely have come to light through advertisements or book reviews in the most important professional journals. And if we expect to find a reference or help in the beautiful volume *Kirchenbau* (Church Building),[227] we will be disappointed. The picture of a native church in the South Sea Islands and a brief discussion by L. Schreyer in his book[228] represent quite a good deal and deserve our gratitude. A few essays might also be mentioned for our orientation.[229]

What, then, do we find if we disregard the use of former heathen temples as churches? Most certainly no one will discover *the* church style. There is none. Nor do we find ourselves in the rather normal stage of experimentation. It is not true that the style of building "has accommodated itself in general to the native style."[230] These are hopes for the future, not facts of the past. The need and fact of experimentation is not recognized only by means of the Christian building style. It is most interesting to note that the new Ramakrishna temple embodies all style forms of the various stages of Indian architecture.[231] There are also two examples to illustrate the use of foreign building styles within the sphere of Buddhism, a fact that appears quite remarkable when we consider the influence Western architecture has exerted on church building. At about the time when Bishop Azariah of Dornakal built his Anglican cathedral, a Buddhist temple was erected in Tsukiji, Tokyo, for which—in our day!—the style of the early Indian temple was chosen in place of the traditional Chinese-Japanese temple style.[237] There is another example from earliest times. Pastor H. Oehler of Tokyo reports on a visit to the great temple mountain Takao-san: "High above the Tokyo plain giant trees three feet in diameter surround an ancient temple of the Buddhist Shingon sect. This sect was led by Kukai from China in 806. This accounts for the thoroughly Chinese appearance of their temples, an impression that becomes especially strong when the 12 protecting deities or the five wisdom deities are placed in bronze or stone figures on a hill beneath or beside the temple. Then it is not difficult to imagine oneself standing in innermost China.[233]

In Afro-Asiatic art three stages of development can be discerned that overlap each other and cannot be separated in point of time. The first is the period of building we might call the Western stage. Nevertheless, there have been notable exceptions even during the earliest beginnings of missionary work, even in the days of the Nestorian mission.[234] Japanese laymen themselves in the 16th century evolved the plans for a three-story church edifice in Japanese style and worthy of the capital city. They also supplied valuable building material and the necessary workmen.[235] Among the pictures made available to us in *Namban Art* is also a color photo of the Kyoto church in Japanese style (No. 157). At this point we also remind the reader of the plans of Matteo Ricci to "build in Chinese style" and of P. Alessandro Valignano, who as far back as 1573 desired that churches be erected in Chinese style for the Chinese, a wish that found early fulfillment.[236]

From the past century the early and earnest efforts of the English Baptists in China must be mentioned.[237] Not so well known is the fact that Robert de Nobili built the first church in Indian style in Madurai.[238] Neither is mention to be omitted of the African cathedral with the thatched roof from the beginning of the 17th century, nor the astonishing aspects of some early churches in Mexico, South America, and in the southern United States, the Catholic cathedral in Phat Diem in Vietnam (1875—1895) in Annam style, and the Anglican Memorial Church of All Saints in Peshawar, Pakistan (1883), in mosque style.[239]

These are gratifying facts, yet in general the missionaries brought their own patterns and church customs into their fields of endeavor, so that it is well-nigh possible to read the history of mission work from the church buildings. "French wedding-cake Gothic," said one critical voice, and another: "Some Japanese churches remind us of Russian village churches."[240] "Completely according to our taste" and "They are equal to the finest (churches) in Spain and Peru" were estimates of churches among the Indians.[241]

Judson Chapel on the university campus in Rangoon "could be a Baptist church erected in any part of the English-speaking world at the close of the 19th century." In the Philippine Islands one Catholic church unfortunately has a "boxlike appearance." In Ceylon Gothic architecture still predominates and Western forms of piety provide "a chronological unity with Western Christendom"; for Anglicans go to church at eleven though Ceylon is in a different time zone and the cooler morning hours would be preferable.[242] Even so distinguished a missionary as Dr. H. Gundert welcomed the fact that in India churches are built in Occidental-Gothic style. Bishop D. Chellappa of Madras knows of the fine architectural specimens in Dornakal, Tirupattur, Erode, and Jaffna and of the chapel of Women's Christian College in Madras. For that reason he deplores it all the more that churches are still being built in "bastard Gothic and in a consciously aggressive foreign style that provokes opposition and even incites contempt. If any change has taken place since 1947, it would doubtless be in the direction of deterioration, especially in those instances in which the decisions were made by the Indian Christians, inasmuch as these gentlemen are frequently more British or American than the Britons and Americans themselves."[243]

On the whole there is agreement that such far-reaching Westernization was not beneficial, but considered from the point of view of the times this was inevitable. So what we deplore today was not done out of ignorance or malice but with good intentions and with the usual good conscience. Our rejection does not constitute condemnation, yet its continuation down to our day is extremely regrettable and should be summarily rejected. And that for several reasons. Perhaps it would suffice to say that in view of modern nationalism and the danger of having the Christian faith stigmatized as something unnecessary and utterly irrelevant, as something alien and imported from the West, no further place can be granted the continuance of such Westernization. Is this misdirected zeal? Is it not a fact that even today foreign control manifests itself in South Korea in the neo-Gothic churches in contrast to older Korean churches? Have we not read Bishop Chellappa's complaint, also that in 1960 large new Gothic churches were being erected in many places in Nigeria? That things could be done differently is stated in the same publication in which the church in Kakindo of Uganda is cited as an example of African art and African architecture and described as an exciting pioneer venture.[244]

Placing both of these factors side by side demonstrates that the second phase does not supersede the first, but that the two, or as we shall see, three phases overlap one another. This is even more true since 1923, when a break occurred. For at that time the papal legate, Archbishop and later Cardinal Celso Costantini, issued the call for the erection of churches in Chinese architecture.[245] Added urgency was thus given to the previously not unknown concern, and the new will to build was confirmed in Catholics as well as in Evangelicals.

The second stage of development, which propelled spontaneous, native, "related to the soil" art into the foreground and strove after the acceptance of ancient, indigenous styles, by no means found a general welcome, nor on the part of all or even the majority of members of the younger churches. By and by however it gained considerable though insufficient ground by means of daring experiments and by exhibits and literary treatment, of which the bibliographies in this author's former and present volumes give an idea.

It cannot be denied that the problem of adaptation which emerges here, a concept borrowed from the field of biology and preferably used in the sense of cultural adaptation—of the adaptation acceptance of indigenous art forms for use by the church—could be dangerous and lead to misgivings.[246]

Since all non-Christian forms have symbolic content and can allow pagan association to arise, caution is needed. There is danger that the newness and the characteristic nature of the new faith could become beclouded and hidden. But are there not dangers everywhere and in every situation? We must become aware of the dangers and attempt to avoid them. The German-American Walther L. Nathan quite properly esposes new ways of building churches. He points to the fact that nothing in Holy Scripture recommends the safe and easy way. "To follow after Jesus means to be ready for change and variation."[247] We must be on the alert! Nothing must be done from fear. Even the strongest determination to do a thing correctly can go awry and bring misfortune. That is regrettable, but we are to learn from it.

Similarly there has never been a safe doctrine or method in the second phase. It has always remained an experiment. That not all attempts have been made known by word and picture is due to this experimenting. This is true primarily of India, where both confessions have ventured many new attempts. It has been mentioned in passing, for example, that in Kalinpong in the eastern Himalaya area there is an impressive church which through its architectonic beauty has become the pride of the district, or that an Indian pastor in a conscious departure from neo-Gothic has built village churches in cruciform as well as Dravidian style.[248] Mention needs to be made that even the experiment in Dornakal has found a critic who is of the opinion that the cathedral missed its mark through its eclecticism and that outwardly it gives the impression of a Russian Orthodox church on the open prairie.[249]

An Anglican source from Korea informs us that the village churches in general have been built in the ancient Korean style. The cathedral of St. Mary and St. Nicolas in Seoul, the first half of which was consecrated as far back as 1926, is said to be the most beautiful church in all Korea, if not in the entire Far East. It was built in such a way that it made no exotic impression on either a Korean or a European, but is "a genuine manifestation of the universal essence of the church." There is a report from the Catholic area concerning a small, picturesque church in Naju which "was erected in pleasing Korean style with slanting roof and eaves turned upward." This is not the only type of church in Korea, for there are many churches, some of them erected quite recently, which are in Gothic and foreign architecture. With their pointed spires they give the impression from afar that one is encountering a most picturesquely situated English village.[250]

With respect to China, Christoph Blumhardt expressed the wish some time ago that a building ought to be somewhat akin to China, and Hudson Taylor expressed himself as being opposed to the "foreign exterior of the chapels" and desired that Christians might worship "in buildings having their own characteristics." "Why must Christianity have a foreign effect?" There are churches of the other type also, and in them the Chinese Christians feel at home.[251] One of them stands opposite Hong Kong. "The church and the entire property is pleasing to the eye, because in this case the architectonic forms of Buddhism, which fit so well into the landscape, have been adopted and given a Christian form." The reference is to Christ Church on the "Mount of the Logos Wind" (Tao Fong Shan), of which we supply a picture (print 133) and about which more is said in the explanation.[252]

The effect a change from a familiar to a foreign building style can have may be learned through an example from Laos. As long as the worship services could be held in the home of a chieftain, attendance and interest were excellent. But when churches were built, both declined. Why? Strangers regard their entrance into a church, unlike that into a home, almost as an identification with an issue or a movement still unknown to them, all the more so if the church in question has a foreign style and represents something foreign and leaves a foreign effect.[253] This impression is still created in Japan, where only a few churches are built in the style of the land.[254] They are, however, very impressive.

Also in Africa efforts are under way to create a national style. In Natal there was at one time a chapel built of sod. "In this plain building without a door or windows, with an altar made of sod, and without a pulpit, I taught the people to sing, to pray, and to understand the divine Word." Just as in Abyssinia the church often had the round form of the inner-African building style, this form of building seems again to commend itself. Unfortunately the reports on such buildings are quite scattered and scarcely understandable to us despite extensive reading. What a novel effect such a building venture can have is demonstrated by this well-nigh frightening statement: "We showed the chapel to our guests, and although (!) it is African in the full meaning of this term, we are proud of it."

As in the seminary for priests in Ibadan, wherever dormitories and lecture halls must be built in the style that is customary and necessary today, the entire plant is nevertheless given an African touch by means of African ornamentation above the entrance.[255]

According to all reports the cathedral in Leopoldville in the Congo appears to be the gem of all African church buildings: "At the spot where the two sections of the city meet there stands a gigantic structure that took my breath away. It was the Cathedral of St. Anne of the Congo. I had never seen such a cathedral. It was a mighty structure that rested on heavy pillars and whose entrance was vaulted over by a stone arch. It stood there between the tall, dark trees, and the glow it reflected had something wild about it. 'Actually it is less a church than a stone hymn to the spirit of the Congo,' I said to my companion.

"The young Frenchman smiled.

"'Exactly! In this cathedral the spirit of the Congo unites itself with the spirit of Christianity. Take a look at this entrance! Of what does it remind you?' With its upward-striving arch it had an almost Gothic effect. Nevertheless it was something different.

"'It looks like a Congo canoe,' I said. 'The entrance with its stone apex resembles a bow.'

"'This is the impression that was intended to be created when the cathedral was erected,' he declared. 'Come, let us go inside.'

"Inside the high-vaulted hall it was dusky and cool. Almost the entire wall behind the altar was covered by a religious scene, quite conventional, it seemed to me. But what attracted my attention most was the heavy stone platform high above our heads. It gave me the impression of being hung and floating up there.

"'That is the place which the choir occupies during the service,' my companion explained, who evidently was much amused by my wonderment.

"'Quite a sizable choir?' I asked.

"'Yes, indeed. Two hundred singers, all Negroes. The cathedral accommodates 5,000 people. Blacks and whites. There is no racial barrier here. I wish you could attend a church service sometime. We carry cultic intermingling quite far. In addition to the choir and an organ we have tomtoms.'"[256]

In addition to churches built in old Western and in native style, more and more are being erected in modern designs. They may have originated in the West, but now they have become thoroughly international, whether we like it or not, whether they are welcomed or deplored. The West itself has given up its traditional building styles in favor of modern techniques. Everyone knows how these modern building styles spread around the world, how they dominate the newly built cities in India, Africa, or Mexico. They are also found in South America as well as in Moscow and Japan. They meet the needs of modern man, and by virtue of their ubiquity are supraracial and truly international. There is today a truly global building style. If it continues to gain ground, if social development on a worldwide basis desires and demands this new art as necessary in connection with its own forms of expression, if in case of radical upheaval and transition the inhabitants of those countries themselves affirm and promote this development and regard it as important for their future, if they move about unhindered in this new environment and feel at home in it—who are we to hinder the Christians in their desire for modern style for their church buildings and sanctuaries? The new style would then correspond precisely to that of their modern dwellings and offices, their public buildings, and their modern means of communication, e.g., the busy airports in Nairobi, Bangkok, and elsewhere. All technical inventions and media are pressed into service regardless of their origin without people considering themselves poor nationalists on that account.

We too, therefore, do not look backward but forward. It would be blind zeal indeed to oppose the juxtaposition of native, modern, and even supermodern architecture. Besides, such building ventures have been undertaken before, as John Butler informs us, even though they gave rise to the suspicion that the West had once more gained a victory over the native and indigenous.[257] The new is not always totally new.

Modern building style must not make everything uniform, tedious, and alike. Walter Gropius is correct in pointing out that modern architecture is sufficiently flexible to take note of and utilize regional variations and to be everything else but anti-native.[258] Climate already compels the architect to engage in fruitful reflection. Native usages and customs dare not be overlooked.[259] There are sufficient examples to illustrate possibilities in the use of variation even in skyscrapers. "The tourist who from his airplane or other elevation views the silhouette of Rio, São Paulo, or Caracas, where 30 or 40 stories are placed vertically one upon another, whereas about two decades ago Colonial Spanish or Portuguese buildings were placed in rows next to each other, imagines that he is seeing Manhattan transported to the South. However, the study of the details, that is, of the essential and the distinctive, quickly erases this impression. Suddenly we discover in these expressionistic symphonies of lines and self-ingratiating colors ... the spirit of an architecture that is ever less ready to share its basic forms with those of the Europeans and Anglo-Saxons. In their place it would conjure up more of the world feeling of the ancient Mayas and Aztecs, as, for example, in the magnificent university city of ancient Mexico, or in the vastness, color intensity, and bizarre contours of South American nature, as in the present capital city Brasilia in the highlands of Goiás.[260]

It is reported from the new China: "In their latest concrete buildings the Chinese have abandoned the ancient forms and in their best performances have developed an architecture that is modern without giving either an ancient or a Western impression by their appearance." The writer, an American, adds concerning the African building style: "We, too, must build well and make use of the best techniques extant, so that the building style will not merely fit into the surroundings but equally into the 20th century."[261] A Catholic warns against the "imported universal style" and exhorts us to strive after simple and pure church buildings and to use native building materials and methods. By falling into line with tradition the mission church runs less danger of becoming a foreign element in the environment. . . . For financial, formal, and ethical reasons church building can never be too simple."[262]

We have not yet given a survey of new church edifices. The few pictures chosen for this book are hardly more than an indication of what is being done. A few data concerning other examples might be desired.[263] It is said concerning the sketch of a Catholic memorial church in Hiroshima that all aggressively modern types are represented in it. The traditional elements remain almost hidden to the hasty viewer. Still they are present. Upon closer inspection they are found embedded in a building style which can be called neither European nor American but universal and modern, yet modified by Japanese influences. It appears that the influences fluctuating between the local, the traditional, and the modern will without question be seen in the coming years in new churches throughout the world."[264]

A small illustrated booklet has been published on the very recent Yamato (Great Peace) Church in Japan. This pretentious building was valued at $250,000. We read in the prospectus that this church was not intended to be an imitation of something European or American, but genuinely Japanese. ... It must be a symbol of the old as well as of the new Japan. Japanese people should be able to feel at home in it. ... The church should not be created for exclusively native interests, but it was to be an ecumenical church. This would make it necessary for the builder to learn from others as well as to make foreign things his own. All the various elements of building would have to be incorporated into this church.[265] What they were aspiring to there has already become a building style in various parts of the world. Of the by no means small number of modern buildings, which include health and congregational centers, we mention the Evangelical church on the island of Ambon,[266] the Anglican Onitsha cathedral in Nigeria, also the Anglican Mbale cathedral in Uganda, the daring plan of the Protestant Episcopal cathedral in Monrovia (Liberia) and the Lutheran church in the same city, the Catholic chapel built before World War II in the village of Pohsarang on the island of Java, and the Catholic church in Ruwe in the Congo.

It is up to the Christians at any given place to determine the building style of a new church. It is also of great importance to consider not merely the financing of large buildings but also and primarily their maintenance.

The way is open to experimentation. Artistic developments cannot be foreseen, yet every Christian, whether African or Asiatic or European or American, must maintain an open mind for surprises, progressiveness, and appreciative tolerance.

But to the Evangelical architects in the Western world and to all who are interested in modern church building we would address the question and the request whether an Evangelical Society of Architects could not be organized, as has been done in the Catholic Church, which would be willing to assist the African churches and brethren by word and deed—and gratis!

That the ornamentation of a church, whether erected in native or modern style, should utilize the various meaningful symbols that are highly regarded by the people of the respective countries should be clear without much proof.[267] Nevertheless, what a person sees in the symbols or what they say to him is not of little consequence. There are many symbols suitable for the pillars, the altar, the baptismal font, and the exterior of the churches. Many of them have already been used to good advantage on and in various churches as well as on the sanctuary chairs and the church pews. They are truly meaningful there. If in the catacombs the peacock was discovered as the symbol of immortality, then the wide use of the banana plant and the lotus in India can be considered quite normal. The lotus appears as a symbol as early as the pre-Portuguese period of India, likewise very early in Chinese and Japanese church work.[268] We refer the reader especially to D. J. Fleming's *Christian Symbols* (New York, 1940).

Also the proper arrangement of Christian burial places is of importance. We offer an example of this in connection with a cemetery of the Zulu Nazareth church in Natal, South Africa. Missionary Otto Dedekind († 1932) gave suggestions for grave care and grave decoration which were soon absorbed into native ideas and forms. As motifs he suggested a cross, a star, and draping, and in 1922 butterflies and flowers made their appearance. The figure of an angel from the year 1932 indicates that the work was original, especially on the part of two brothers who took a special interest in the matter. According to the Zulu Christians this was the angel that rolled away the stone from Jesus' sepulcher. On tombstones from 1938 and 1939 the sun and the tree of life are used as symbols of the resurrection (prints 28 and 29). All producers and craftsmen were Zulus. Our authority for this found similar motifs at distant preaching places. The figures are chiseled in and painted over with one or more natural colors that stand up against the weather. The art of producing tombstones continues to be developed, though the newer stones do not compare in beauty with those that were produced in the aforementioned years. This report and the missing reports on cemetery and grave care in other parts of Africa and in other countries seem to indicate that this area—which also takes on a witnessing characteristic—ought to be included in the general promotion of art cultivation in Africa and Asia.[269]

The Empty Hands

The artist knows the status of the empty hands. Indian books on the theory of art require that the master should paint only after long meditation and from the deepest inspiration. When a Japanese, a master of Zen Buddhism, saw a landscape by Caspar David Friedrich in Tokyo, he was moved. Finally he asked a question, but not a question concerning connections with historical art and the like. He asked: "Was he through?"

When asked by the German owner of the picture: "What do you mean by 'through'?" he unfolded the three-word question with three questions: "Was he still afraid of death? Did he see sense in nonsense? Was he standing under the banner of universal love?"[270]

Actual life does not always correspond to lofty goals. "In practice it was as with us," reads the translation of this ancient Indian axiom. Nevertheless it is of supreme importance that there be a goal which directs us downward and upward.

We would like to see the Christian artist as an "artist *coram Deo*" (in the presence of God).[271] We cannot look into anyone's heart. Whether he is weak or strong in faith, whether driven about by doubts or firmly grounded, the Christian artist must participate in the life of worship and create out of faith. Not all African and Asiatic artists whose names are mentioned in this book have made statements with regard to their faith life and church connections. Some did so, and for this reason the voices of those may become audible here who stood before their God with empty hands.

The Catholic Yamamoto confessed: "For that reason I always prepare myself for my work by prayer."

Angelo Da Fonseca is a practicing Catholic Christian.

The Indians L. R. Patole and S. S. Bundellu said in their letters: "My supreme goal is to serve God with my art," and: "I have dedicated my art exclusively to Biblical themes."[272] Other creative artists have likewise written to the author and emphasized strongly that they belong to this or that church and are a part of congregational life. A few have also allowed this to come out in personal conversation.

The African nun Ancilla of Southern Rhodesia closes her report on her plastic work thus: "This talent is a gift of God." And the Chinese Monica Liu Ho-Peh could write: "If the heart is right, spirit and hand are in harmony. The spirit is mirrored in the painting and has its seat in the point of the brush. The painter of religious art must have a sincere faith and a deep artistic talent in order to execute his art. . . . I cannot be happy if I do not serve God, the Only One. I paint for God."[273]

It is not a new insight that Afro-Asiatic art is a sure sign of spiritual life in the younger churches. It serves in proclaiming the Good News to Christians and non-Christians; it is missionary art in a twofold sense. As Kurt Goldammer has shown, it resembles "early Christian art as missionary art."[274]

The purpose of this book and, above all, of its picture section is to invite the reader to take note of these expressions of art. The pictures at least offer the possibility of gaining an impression of art in the ecumenical church. Should the church and the world of art become aware of this art, much would be gained for the cause of art and its creators. Experts will find it difficult, if not impossible, to gain an awareness of it without comparing and evaluating. We are not opposed to that nor to criticism; in fact, we have asked for it. Naturally we want to caution against premature criticism, because we are dealing with an art for whose proper evaluation and appreciation certain presuppositions must be present in a viewer from the Western countries. In writing this our thoughts instincively revert to a warning example of a premature utterance. We are thinking of Prof. F. von Luschan, who published the *Altertümer von Benin* (Antiquities of Benin). Of him it is stated: "Had he simply published a descriptive and illustrated catalog of the Benin Antiquities, which have become known, he would have earned our gratitude for a meritorious collection. . . . But he went far beyond this goal." We then read that a man with a great capacity for empathy would have been required, but he was not the man. For a time he engaged in interpretations and speculations that disallowed empathy and for which he did not possess the necessary range of knowledge.[275]

Neither the viewer nor the author cares to become a victim of the same mistake and subject to the same verdict by a future that possesses greater knowledge. The author desires to be no more than a collector who points to the artistic work in the African and Asiatic congregations which, like those in other countries, endeavor to mount the jewel of faith in vessels worthy of it.

Also our hands are empty to receive.

A Necessary Postscript

The Hayas in Tanzania say: "He who does not thank, discourages the giver."

I must thank the kind givers, even if I were not permitted to hope that "whoever thanks, encourages the giver." My collection of testimonies to Christian art from the ecumenical church owes its growth in the number of books and in the existence of considerably more than a thousand slides not only to my personal endeavors as a collector but also to many known as well as personally unknown patrons and friends who have sent me pictures, photographs, and printed material. To say a cordial, public "Thank you" to all who in the fullest sense of the word are at home in all the world is a sincere "must" on my part. These heartfelt thanks are directed particularly to all the artists in Africa and Asia whose names appear in this book only in passing. I am equally grateful to all persons, editors, and official sources mentioned in the Source of Pictures section for permission to reproduce the pictures.

For the translation of the legends for the pictures I asked the following gentlemen to serve: Rev. Paul Hoffmann, Geneva; Rev. Bror Tiliander, M.A., B.D., Coimbatore, S. India; editor-in-chief Yves Chabas, Lyon; and theol. cand. Peter Lobers, Halle (Saale). To all of them my heartfelt thanks for their friendly and prompt assistance.

The arrangement of the pictures was made according to the alphabetical sequence of countries adopted by the United Nations. Within individual countries and continents the procedure in general was to arrange the pictures according to the names of the artists, followed by pictures of unknown artists, and then buildings.

That at times no precise data could be supplied is a source of regret first and foremost to the author. He therefore would voice the request at this time—for the benefit of all scientifically interested persons as well as our readers and viewers—that for the published pictures and charts data concerning the artist, and the architect, as well as the time and country of their origin, be forwarded wherever possible. This would assist one and all toward a better understanding of the art of the ecumenical church. To Dr. Theo Lehmann, science assistant at Martin Luther University in Halle-Wittenberg, I express my sincere thanks for his manifold support and cooperation in the preparation of the manuscript. I also thank science assistant Rudolf Göbel for his help in proofreading.

Halle (Saale), December 1965   Arno Lehmann

Notes

1. *Theol. Zeitschrift der Theol. Fak. der Universität Basel*, XIV (1958), 73.

2. *The Hibbert Journal*, LVI (July 1958), 387.

3. *Indian Culture and the Fullness of Christ, All India Study Week* (Dec. 6—13, 1956); Madras, 1957.

4. *Katholisches Missionsjahrbuch der Schweiz* (Freiburg, 1958), p. 76.

5. Cf. Nos. 170 and 175 of Bibliography.

6. *National Christian Council Review*, Nagpur, India, LXXIX, 8 (Sept. 1959), 347f.; ibid., LXXXII, 8 (Aug. 1962), 308f. Hereafter *NCC Review*.

7. Evangelical Literature Depot, P.O. Box 2340, Calcutta 1.

8. 475 Riverside Drive, New York, N.Y. 10027.

9. *Introduction and Catalog of the Municipal Art Museum*, Recklinghausen, "Negro Art and Christianity" (March 9—April 22, 1957); *S.S.H.M. Musical Bulletin*, I, 2 (Allahabad, 1961), 27; *Japan ruft* (Bremen, Dec. 1959), p. 43.

10. German: *Evangelische Missions-Zeitschrift* (Hamburg, 1960), p. 39, Hereafter *EMZ*.

11. B. de Rachewiltz, *Afrikanische Kunst* (Zurich and Stuttgart, 1960), pp. 174—87; Ferdinand Herrmann, *Beiträge zur afrikanischen Kunst* (Berlin, 1958), p. 10; F. Elger and R. Maillard, *Picasso* (Munich and Zurich, 1956), pp. 48, 61, 74, 88, 101, 267; A. Locke, *The New Negro* (New York, 1925), pp. 258, 261.

12. (Brunswick, 1960), pp. 67, 295.

13. Rachewiltz, p. 190.

14. Ibid., pp. 192, 198.

15. (Mannheim, 1957), pp. 16, 19.

16. Prints 6—9, 11, 25—28, 33, 39.

17. *Neue Zeitschrift für Missionswissenschaft*, XVI, 3 (1960), 223f. Hereafter *NZM*.

18. (Madras, 1953), Nos. 42, 62—63, 102, 129.

19. (London, 1958), pp. 161f.

20. *NZM*, pp. 222, 225.

21. *Christliche Kunst des XX. Jahrhunderts* (Hamburg, 1959), prints 5, 12, 17, 19, 38.

22. Ibid., pp. 34, 64—65, 69, 148.

23. P. Regamey, Graz, Vienna, Cologne (1954), prints 78—79; in the text, pp. 71, 183, 499.

24. W. L. Nathan, Philadelphia (1961). In support of the self-evident presupposition that a general book title in Europe or in Germany can only and exclusively mean "our art" and should be thus understood despite different expectations, we might also mention A. Neumeyer, *Die Kunst in unserer Zeit, Versuch einer Deutung* (Stuttgart, 1961), and R. Schwarz, *Kirchenbau* (Heidelberg, 1960).

25. H. E. Bahr, *Poiesis, theol. Untersuchung der Kunst* (Stuttgart, 1961).

26. Ibid., pp. 103, 105.

27. *Das Buch von drüben, Information für Bücherfreunde*, No. 4 (1957), p. 19.

28. *The Examiner*, July 13, 1957, p. 349.

29. *NZM*, p. 225.

30. E. Elisofon, *The Sculpture of Africa* (London, 1958), pp. 23f.

31. *Bulletin der Indischen Botschaft*, Bonn, IX, 5 (May 1959), 4. The speaker was the then Indian ambassador Badr-ud-Din Tjabji.

32. *Bible illustrée par Simon Segal; Bible illustrée par Léopold Marboef; Bible en Imagesm de Véronique Filozof*. These and the two missals mentioned: Labergerie, Paris, 1957, 1955 resp.

33. *Jesus Christ, An Illustrated Life of Christ* (London, 1962); original Dutch edition published by Uitgeverij De Toorts (Haarlem, 1961).

34. *Illustrated Weekly of India*, March 1960, p. 3. Cf. also J. Weber, "Vom Wesen der künstlerischen Aussage," *Pastoraltheologie*, Göttingen, XLV, 10 (1956), 385—97. "Today we can hardly speak of a consensus regarding the nature of art. That which some regard as the greatest art is called trash by others; that for which some pay thousands, others consider worthless. Many different tendencies exist side by side in the field of art, and a Babylonian confusion of opinion dominates the daily discussion of it. Nor can it by any means be said that the much-discussed difference of opinion exists only between art connoisseurs and laymen. Indeed not, for even distinguished art connoisseurs who all their lifetime have occupied themselves with the study and pursuit of art arrive at completely opposite opinions. If in the course of time agreement has been reached among them on some points, the conflict of opinions nevertheless remains frightening." (Weber, p. 386)

35. Quoted in W. Busch, Rev. Dr. Busch, Elmshorn 1941[4], p. 158.

36. J. Specker and W. Bühlmann, *Das Laienapostolat in den Missionen. Festschrift für Joh. Beckmann* (Schöneck-Beckenried, 1961), p. 60.

37. Fr. F. van Trigt, S.M.A., *Negerkunst und Christentum*, City Art Museum catalog (Recklinghausen, 1957), p. 4.

38. Ibid., p. 3.

39. *Die nackten Nagas* (Leipzig, 1947), pp. 73f.

40. *Machet zu Jüngern alle Völker* (Freiburg, 1962), pp. 589, 704; J. Hofinger et al., *Worship: The Life of the Missions* (Notre Dame, Ind., 1958), p. 199.

41. *Die nackten Nagas*, pp. 69, 74f.

42. *The Illustrated Weekly of India*, July 17, 1960, p. 55.

43. *Africa South* (Cape Town), II, 4 (July—Sept. 1958), 98f.

44. *African Art* (Zurich and Stuttgart, 1960), pp. 192, 198.

45. L. Kohl-Larsen, *Die Bildstraße Ostafrikas, Felsbilder in Tanzania* (Kassel, 1958), p. 6.

46. F. van Trigt, pp. 4f.

47. *Machet zu Jüngern alle Völker*, pp. 704, 716.

48. *Muntu, an Outline of Neo-African Culture* (London, 1961), pp. 177f; *Muntu, Umrisse der neo-afrikanischen Kultur* (Düsseldorf, 1958), pp. 182f. Cf. also E. Elisofon, p. 162; H. U. Beier, "Christliche Kunst in Nigeria," *Frankfurter Allgemeine Zeitung*, Dec. 21, 1957, No. 296, feature page; A. Loescher, "Schnitzerschule von Serima in Rhodesien," *Die Katholischen Missionen*, June 1960, pp. 84—87; Picture of the president's chair in the Parliament in Ibadan (photo by Carrol), *Die Katholischen Missionen*, Dec. 1960, p. 207; "Neuguinea-Schnitzerei," Wilhelm Fiegmann, *Junge Kirche zwischen Steinzeit und Neuzeit* (Neuendettelsau, 1959), pp. 44f.

49. Cf. pamphlet *And Was Made Man*, with an introduction by Mrs. K. M. Trowell and 12 prints (London, 1960).

50. *Neue Kunst in Afrika*, pp. 20—25.

51. *Die Katholischen Missionen*, No. 6 (1961), pp. 191 to 196.

52. *Cyrene, Africans in the Making* (London, 1949).

53. Ibid., pp. 12f.

54. London, S.P.G., no date, with "some notes of the artists."

55. *Africa South*, II, 4 (July—Sept. 1958), 106—108.

56. F. Klemann, *Europäer und Ostasiaten* (Munich and Basel, 1957), p. 197.

57. *Die Katholischen Missionen*, Dec. 1961, p. 191; No. 3, 1960.

58. St. Neill, *The Unfinished Task* (London, 1957), p. 120.

59. *Weltkirche und Weltreligionen* (Freiburg, 1960), p. 83.

60. *The Relation between the Younger and the Older Churches*, III (London, 1928), 166.

61. *International Review of Missions*, XLVII, 186 (April 1958), 146. Hereafter IRM.

62. *Der Grosse Entschluss*, Vienna, IX (Feb. 1954), 143. After completing the manuscript I came upon an unsupported assertion which, however, is to be accepted. In an essay on "Council and Mission" Archabbot Suso Brechter, O.S.B., St. Ottilia, writes concerning a statement of a native priest in Tanzania that the natives do not want an African Christianity, but Roman Catholic Christianity expressed in a distinctively African manner. A few lines later he adds: "Looking back, one must admit in all candor that efforts made from a lofty viewpoint by the then Cardinal Castantini to create a Christian-Chinese art, which at the time were greeted with great optimism in certain circles, were in reality 'beating the air,' in fact, failures. The council will probably also tackle this ticklish matter." *Die Katholischen Missionen*, LXXXI, 5 (Oct. 1962), 148.

63. J. B. Aufhauser, "Christliche einheimische Kunst in nichtchristlichen Ländern," *Die Christliche Kunst*, XXV (1928—29), 161f.

64. For the Catholic view cf. T. Ohm, *Machet zu Jüngern alle Völker* (Freiburg, 1962), Index.

65. *Una Sancta*, Meitingen near Augsburg, XV, 4 (Dec. 1960), 286.

66. *Illustrated Weekly of India*, July 17, 1960, p. 47.

67. *Ökumenischer Pressedienst*, Geneva, XXVII, 43 (Nov. 18, 1960), 1. Cf. also P. D. Devanandan, *The Gospel and Renascent Hinduism* (London, 1959), pp. 33, 56.

68. *How I found God and how God found me*, Ramanreti, 1952[2], p. 193.

69. Quoted in the weekly *Star*, Djarkata, Dec. 26, 1959.

70. H. Mukarowsky, *Africa, Geschichte und Gegenwart* (1961), p. 242.

71. A. M. Thunberg, *Kontinente im Aufbruch* (1960), pp. 43, 46, 53.

72. Ibid., pp. 68f.

73. Ps. 65:10.

74. *Neue Kunst in Afrika*, p. 25f.

75. *Muntu*, English, p. 179; German, p. 184.

76. Ibid., English, pp. 181f.; German, p. 186.

77. *World Cultures and World Religions* (London, 1960), pp. 18, 159.

78. Tei Nishimura (Tokyo, 1960).

79. *Indian Journal of Theology*, V, 2 (Oct. 1956), 19; *Neue Zeit*, No. 73 (March 27, 1957), p. 4.

80. *Neue Zeit*, loc. cit.

81. *Das Eine Buch*, No. 10 (June 1959).

82. *Bulletin of the United Bible Societies*, No. 38, pp. 71f.

83. E. Elisofon, p. 163.

84. *The Life of Christ* (London, 1948). These pictures are also in *Die Kunst der Jungen Kirchen*.

85. Th. B. W. G. Gramberg, letter dated June 4, 1959.

86. S. S. Bundellu, letter dated July 24, 1959.

87. *Zeichen der Zeit*, No. 3 (1957), pp. 123f.

88. Ibid., p. 124.

89. *The Unifinished Task* (London, 1957), p. 120.

90. F. Dean Lueking, letter dated Aug. 12, 1960.

91. *Kunst und Kirche*, XX, 4 (1957), 190; *Neue Zeit*, loc. cit.

92. Quoted in *Das Gottesbild im Abendland*, p. 157.

93. E.g., *IRM*, L, 198 (April 1961), 184f.

94. *Lutherischer Rundblick*, Oberursel, IX, 4 (1961), 200.

95. Dr. Dexter C. Ogan, letter dated July 23, 1960.

96. A. Locke, *The New Negro, an Interpretation* (New York, 1925), pp. 264 f.; L. Hughes, *Famous American Negroes* (New York, 1954), pp. 63—65.

97. W. L. Nathan, *Art and the Message of the Church* (Philadelphia, 1961), p. 141.

98. *Die Katholischen Missionen*, No. 6, (1957).

99. Dr. Idowu of the University College in Ibadan demanded at the first conference of the Reformed World Council on African soil (Aug. 1962) before 100 Reformed delegates that the church must oppose the present-day equation of missions and colonial exploitation also by discarding its characteristically European traits. *ÖPD*, Geneva, XXIX, 31 (Aug. 31, 1962), 3.

100. *NZM*, XVI, 4 (1960), 305.

101. Rev. 22:19.

102. Eccl. 3:14.

103. Phil. 1:18.

104. W. Schöne et al., *Das Gottesbild im Abendland* (Witten and Berlin, 1959); U. Steffen, "Das Bild als theologisches Problem," *Pastoraltheologie*, XLIII, 9 (Sept. 1959), 364—70; H. Frhr. v. Campenhausen, "Die Bilderfrage in der Reformation, *Zeitschrift für Kirchengeschichte*, ser. 4, VI, Vol. 68, 1—2, pp. 96 to 128; P. Althaus, "Die Illustration der Bibel als theologisches Problem," *Neue Zeitschrift für Systematische Theologie*, I, 2—3 (1959), 314—26; K. Lüthi, "Bildende Kunst als theologisches Problem," *Theologische Zeitschrift*, Basel, No. 2 (1960), pp. 120—32; Bahr, *Poiesis*, cf. Index; K. H. Bernhardt, *Gott und Bild* (Berlin, 1956); L. Schreyer, *Christliche Kunst des XX. Jahrhunderts* (Hamburg, 1959), pp. 64, 122, 143 f.; *Die Religion in Geschichte und Gegenwart*, 3d ed. (Tübingen: J. C. B. Mohr, 1957), I, cols. 1275 f.; *Glaube und Bild, Festschrift für A. Wider*, Widnau, Switzerland (1960).

105. *Kirchliche Dogmatik*, II, 1, 751.

106. H. Flügel, *Radius*, No. 2 (1957), pp. 38—42.

107. P. Althaus, p. 322.

108. L. Schreyer, p. 122.

109. H. Flügel, p. 42.

110. *Theologische Literaturzeitung*, No. 9 (1960), col. 684.

111. *Luther's Works*, American Edition, 40, pp. 99—100.

112. *Christliche Kunst*, p. 64.

113. J. Jahn, *Muntu*, English, pp. 182 f.; German, pp. 187 f.

114. A. Campbell, *Afrika—Gesicht und Seele* (Stuttgart, 1954), p. 394.

115. *Africa South* (July—Sept. 1958), pp. 99 f.

116. F. J. Dölger, "Die Sonne der Gerechtigkeit und der Schwarze," *Liturgiegeschichtliche Forschungen*, No. 2 (1918), pp. 49—75.

117. P. Sulzer, *Schwarze Intelligenz* (Zurich, 1955), p. 39.

118. J. V. Taylor and D. Lehmann, *Christians of the Copperbelt* (London, 1961), p. 139.

119. Pearl S. Buck, *This Proud Heart* (New York, 1938).

120. *The Foreign Missionary*, New York (March 1958), p. 5.

121. *Die Katholischen Missionen*, No. 1 (1961), pp. 31 f.

122. In the poem "Nativity" by the Fanti Negress Aquah Laluah (born 1904), *The Poetry of the Negro, 1746—1949*, ed. Langston Hughes and Arna Bontemps (New York, 1956), p. 384. On the Christian-European influence on the African representation of the Mother and Child cf. O. Nuoffer, *Afrikanische Plastik in der Gestaltung von Mutter und Kind* (Dresden, no date), pp. 62 ff., 18—19.

123. *Der Große Entschluß*, Vienna, IX (Feb. 1954), 144.

124. J. Jahn, English, p. 178; German, p. 182.

125. J. V. Taylor and D. Lehmann, p. 190.

126. Quoted in *Theologisches Jahrbuch 1959* (Leipzig, 1959), pp. 351 f.

127. E. Erkes, "Ein chinesisch-katholisches Heiligenbild," *Jahrbuch des Museums für Völkerkunde zu Leipzig*, XV, (Berlin, 1956), pp. 31 f.; "Zur Einwirkung der Madonna auf die afrikanische Mutter-Kind-Darstellung" cf. P. Germann, *Beiträge zur afrikanischen Kunst* (Berlin, 1958), pp. 49, 56.

128. A. Locke, *The New Negro* (New York, 1925), pp. 252 f. In the Ras Tafari cult in Jamaica they speak of "our beloved black Creator." IRM, LI, 204 (Oct. 1962), 474.

129. Cf. the pertinent chapter in Th. Lehmann, *Negro Spirituals, Geschichte und Theologie* (Berlin, 1965), pp. 200 f.

130. Die Kunst der Jungen Kirchen, S. 44 f.

131. Quoted from *Jahresbericht der Breklumer Mission* (1961—62), p. 7.

132. A voice from Pakistan says "that all criticism of Christianity always applies only to the foreign forms in which the church appears." *Die Katholischen Missionen*, LXXXI, 5 (Oct. 1962), 154; J. V. Taylor and D. Lehmann, ibid., p. 189.

133. Print 11 in R. Italiaander, *Neue Kunst in Afrika*.

134. *The Christian Century*, LXXIX, 32 (Aug. 8, 1962), 971.

135. B. Sundkler, "Bantu Messiah and White Christ," *Practical Anthropology*, VII, 4 (July—Aug. 1960), 170 f. Cf. also B. Sundkler, *Bantu Prophets in South Africa* (London, 1948); G. Linnenbrink, "Der afrikanische Nationalimus und seine theologische Problematik," under "Schwarzer Zionismus," p. 73, *EMZ*, XIX, 2 (July 1962); E. Andersson, *Messianic Popular Movements in the Lower Congo* (Uppsala, 1958); C. de Mestral, "Christianity and African Separatist Churches in South Africa," *Occasional Papers* (IMC), London, No. 4 (Jan. 1960).

136. K. Schlosser, *Eingeborenenkirchen in Süd- und Südwestafrika* (Kiel, 1958), pp. 39, 242.

137. D. Bonhoeffer, *Ethik* (Munich, 1949), p. 60.

138. W. A. Visser't Hooft, ed. *New Delhi 1961* (Stuttgart, 1962), p. 494.

139. Ibid., p. 496.

140. *Message and Mission* (New York, 1960), p. 177.

141. *World Cultures and World Religions* (London, 1961), pp. 133.

142. *The Christian Faith and Non-Christian Religions* (Digswell Place, 1958), pp. 206—23.

143. Ibid., p. 221.

144. *Christianity in the Indian Crucible* (Calcutta, 1957), p. 158.

145. *The Life of the Buddha* (no publisher, place, or date). Cf. A. Rosenberg, ed. *Christentum und Buddhismus* (Munich-Planegg, 1959), p. 125.

146. *Oriental Press*, Manila (no date).

147. Cf. *The Lutheran Hymnal* (St. Louis, 1941), No. 80.

148. W. Oehler, *Aufstand in China* (Hamburg, 1958), p. 87.

149. H. Wolf, *Indisches Bilderbuch zum Leben Jesu* (Stuttgart, 1955), p. 7.

150. *Nachrichten aus der Bethel-Mission*, Nos. 11, 12 (1956), pp. 146—48.

151. *Die Kunst der Jungen Kirchen*, pp. 22—26.

152. *The Student World*, Geneva, XLVIII, 2 (1955).

153. Ibid., pp. 147, 155.

154. H. Kraemer, *Religion and the Christian Faith* (London, 1956), p. 410; German ed., *Religion und Christlicher Glaube* (Göttingen, 1959), p. 403.

155. W. T. Thomas and R. B. Manikam, *The Church in Southeast Asia* (New York, 1956), p. 38.

156. Berlin and Bielefeld, 1951.

157. Ethel E. Wallis, *The Dayuma Story: Life Under Auca Spears* (New York, 1960), p. 250; *Practical Anthropology*, Supplement 1960, p. 60.

158. Devanesen Rajarigam, Gütersloh and Berlin, 1961. Cf. my review in *Theol. Lit. Zeitung*, No. 4 (1962), cols. 306—308.

159. IV, 1 (Spring 1953, New York), pp. 17f.

160. *Die Katholischen Missionen*, No. 2 (1958), pp. 35 to 40.

161. Ibid., No. 2 (1957), pp. 35—38.

162. *The Christian Mission Among Rural People* (New York, 1945).

163. *Message and Mission* (New York, 1960), p. 176; *Practical Anthropology*, VII, 5 (1960), 202; J. Collier, *Indians of the Americas* (New York, 1947), p. 49; NZM, XV, 4 (1959), 308.

164. T. Ohm, *Das Katechumenat in den Katholischen Missionen* (Münster, 1959), pp. 76f.

165. *The Student World*, XLVII, 2 (1955), 117f., 153.

166. W. Ruben, *Einführung in die Indienkunde* (Berlin, 1954), p. 97.

167. V. Cronin, *A Pearl of India, the Life of R. de Nobili* (New York, 1959), pp. 185, 264.

168. *NZM*, XVI, 2 (1960), 100f.

169. *NCC Review*, LXXXII, 6—7 (1962), 249; H. Thomä, *Frauen in fernen Ländern* (Stuttgart, 1958), p. 146.

170. S. Müller, *Ärzte helfen in aller Welt* (Stuttgart, 1957), p. 177.

171. June 22, 1958, pp. 36f.

172. *NCC Review*, loc. cit.; IRM, LI, 204 (Oct. 1962), 460—70; *Bulletin of the United Bible Societies*, No. 52, 4 (1962), p. 147.

173. *Das Laienapostolat in den Missionen* (Schöneck-Beckenried, 1961), pp. 329f.

174. P. Vittoz, *Goldene Dächer—Schwarze Zelte* (Constance, 1958), p. 178.

175. *EMZ*, 1959, p. 85.

176. *Die Katholischen Missionen*, No. 2 (1958), pp. 61f.

177. M. Berndt, "*Adaptation of the Religious Dance*," pp. 249, 267—70 (for details cf. n. 185); Msgr. J. Malenfant, "Catholic School and Indian Culture." *Catholicus*, March 1954.

178. J. V. Taylor, "The Development of African Drama for Education and Evangelism, *IRM*, XXXIX (July 1950), 292—301; NZM, XIV, 1 (1958), 147; E. and M. Ross, *Africa Disturbed* (New York, 1959), pp. 160f.; H. Thomä, pp. 121, 187; *Der Auftrag*, Stuttgart (Dec. 1958), p. 166.

179. *Die Katholischen Missionen*, No. 2 (1960), pp. 69f.

180. Chr. Kaiser Verlag (Munich, 1957).

181. *Das Laienapostolat*, p. 338.

182. *In alle Welt*, Neuendettelsau, No. 12 (1956), title page.

183. *Die Kunst der Jungen Kirchen*, p. 23.

184. E. Steinborn, *Die Kirchenzucht in der Geschichte der deutschen evangelischen Mission* (Leipzig, 1928), pp. 28, 33, 91f.; *IRM*, XLVII (April 1958), 222f.; J. Ilsen, *Auch ich bin ein Mensch* (Frankfurt/M., 1960²), p. 151.

185. M. Berndt, "Adaptation of the Religious Dance and Similar Physical Movements in the Indigenous Church" (St. Louis, Mo.: Concordia Seminary, 1960), mimeographed.

186. M. Warren, *Revival* (London, 1954), p. 30.

187. NZM, XV, 1 (1959), 56f.

188. E. and M. Ross, *Africa Disturbed*, (New York, 1959), p. 163.

189. *Schwarze Macht* (Hamburg, 1956), pp. 121—23, 200.

190. Quoted from IRM, XVI (July 1956), 259. Concerning the relation of religion to dance cf. G. van der Leeuw, *Vom Heiligen in der Kunst* (Gütersloh, 1957), pp. 25, 35, 38, 40f., 43, 45, 48, 50, 61, 73, 79; also

Fr. Heyer, *Der Tanz in der Modernen Gesellschaft* (Hamburg, 1958), pp. 141, 143, 146f., 152.

191. L. P. Aujulat, *Afrika kommt* (Munich, 1960), 39.

192. Berndt, p. 165.

193. *Das Wort in der Welt*, Hamburg, No. 4 (1960), p. 60.

194. R. De Coccola, Paul King, *Ayorama* (Freiburg-Munich, 1959), pp. 236f.

195. *Die Katholischen Missionen*, No. 3 (1961), p. 91.

196. C. Keysser, *Lehret alle Völker* (Neuendettelsau, 1960), pp. 16, 81, 83; G. Pilhofer, *Die Geschichte der Neuendettelsauer Mission in Neuguinea* (Neuendettelsau, 1961), pp. 157, 169, 211; *Das Wort in der Welt* (Hamburg, 1960), p. 60; *Bayrisches Sonntagsblatt*, Munich, May 22, 1955. Cf. also C. Andresen "Altchristliche Kritik am Tanz, ein Ausschnitt aus dem Kampf der alten Kirche gegen heidnische Sitte," *Zeitschrift für Kirchengeschichte*, LXXII (1961), 217—62.

197. C. Devanesen, *The Cross Is Lifted* (New York, 1954), p. 11; E. Asirvatham, *Christianity in the Indian Crucible* (Calcutta, 1957), p. 170.

198. *Des Katechumenat*, p. 77.

199. *NCC Review*, LXXX, 8 (1960), 276, 280; ibid., LXXXI, 9 (1961), 299, 302; Blaise Levau, ed. *Revolution in Missions* (Calcutta, 1958²), p. 137; B. Hürtgen, "Sakraler Tanz (neue Versuche)," *Zeitschrift für Missions- und Religionswissenschaft*, No. 41 (1957), pp. 193 to 200; H. Volken, "Szenen des Evangeliums im indischen Tanz," ibid., No. 40 (1956), pp. 165f. T. Ohm also mentions Edmond, *Gospel Scenes in Indian Dance* (Allahabad), but without details, which I am unable to supply.

200. Quoted in G. Vicedom, *Das Abendmahl in den jungen Kirchen* (Munich, 1960), p. 31.

201. *Stimme der Orthodoxie*, No. 6 (Berlin, 1962), pp. 9f.

202. R. Italiaander, *Tanz in Afrika* (Berlin, 1960).

203. H. Weman, "The sacral dance," *African Music and Church in Africa* (Uppsala, 1960), pp. 195—98.

204. *Kunst und Kirche*, XXV, 2 (1962), p. 84.

205. H. J. Margull, *Aufbruch zur Zukunft* (Gütersloh, 1962), p. 84; B. A. Pauw, *Religion in a Tswana Chiefdom* (London, 1960), p. 201.

206. Berndt, p. 135; Nida, *Message and Mission*, p. 175.

207. Taylor, *Christians of the Copperbelt*, pp. 106, 218f., D. A. McGavran, *How Churches Grow* (London, 1959), p. 159.

208. G. Günther, *Erweckung in Afrika* (Stuttgart, 1959), p. 28.

209. *Prelude to Ghana* (London, 1957), p. 10; M. Warren, *Revival* (London, 1954), p. 65.

210. J. S. Trimingham, *The Christian Church and Islam in West Africa* (London, 1955), pp. 49, 36.

211. J. F. Ewing, ed. *Social Action in Mission Lands* (New York, 1955), p. 147.

212. *Berichte aus der Rheinischen Mission*, No. 12 (Wuppertal-Barmen, 1960), p. 231.

213. Berndt, p. 135f.; Warren, p. 66.

214. *Schwarze Macht*, p. 65 and p. 108.

215. *African Music and the Church in Africa*, Bibliography, pp. 291—96. On African Music and the African roots of the Negro Spirituals cf. also *Das Buch der Spirituals and Gospel Songs* (Hamburg, 1961), pp. 155ff.; cf. also "Music in the Missions: Its Importance, Its Qualities, Its Functions in Worship, the Liturgical Arts in the Missions," J. Hofinger et al., *Worship: The Life of the Missions* (Notre Dame, Ind.: University of Notre Dame Press, 1958), chs. 13—16.

216. *Magazine Souvenir of Summer School of Hindustani Music* (Allahabad, 1959), p. 20.

217. *NCC Review*, LXXVIII, 2 (1958), 84.

218. Nida, *Message and Mission*, p. 175.

219. Loc. cit.; B. Sundkler, *The Christian Ministry in Africa*, (London, 1962), p. 121.

220. *S.S.H.M. Musical Bulletin* (Allahabad, 1960), p. 4.

221. Ibid., p. 17.

222. *The Foreign Missionary*, New York, March 1958, p. 10; *Mitteilungen der Norddeutschen Mission*, Bremen, No. 2 (1961), pp. 1f.

223. J. Ilsen, *Auch ich bin ein Mensch*, p. 150; *Practical Anthropology*, V, 5—6 (1958), 218.

224. H. de Kleine, ed. ... *gemacht zu Seinem Volk* (Wuppertal-Barmen, 1961), p. 15; ibid., on the singing of the Batak congregations, pp. 69ff., 92, 102, 109, 114f.

225. *Die Katholischen Missionen*, LXXIX, 5 (1960), 159—62.

226. *Die Religion in Geschichte und Gegenwart*, III, cols. 1410—11; *Kunst der jungen Kirchen*, pp. 45—52.

227. R. Schwarz, *Kirchenbau* (Heidelberg, 1960).

228. *Christliche Kunst des XX. Jahrhunderts*, print 5 and pp. 58f.; 163f.

229. *Katholisches Missionsjahrbuch der Schweiz* (Freiburg, 1958), p. 76: *Art d'église*, XXVII, 4, 241—67; *Kunst und Kirche*, XXV (Feb. 1962), 81—89; *Glaube und Bild*, Widnau, Switzerland, pp. 138—44; *DWM News Letter*, Geneva, Lutheran World Federation, No. 9 (1950), pp. 9—17; K. Freuler, "Vom Kirchenbauen in der Mission," *Die Katholischen Missionen*, June 1959, pp. 171—74; E. Ladner, "Kirchenbau in der Mission," *Kath. Missionsjahrbuch der Schweiz 1962* ("Kunst, Kult, Kontinente"), pp. 78f., prints, pp. 76f., "Plan und Modell der Kirche in Koumi, Ober-Volta, mit Erläuterung," pp. 80ff.; J. Butler, "The Theology of Church Building in India, *Indian Journal of Theology*, V (Feb. 1956), 1—20 (contains a good bibliography); "Further Thoughts on Architecture in India," ibid., VIII, 4/VIII (April 1959), 135—50 (lit.); "19 Centuries of Christian Missionary Architecture," *Journal of the Society of Architectural Historians*, XXI, 1 (1962), 3—17 (lit. and prints); "Modernist Art in the Younger

Churches, typescript in *Wort und Antwort, Festschrift für Arno Lehmann,* 1961; T. Ohm, *Machet zu Jüngern alle Völker,* pp. 717f. 230. *EMZ* (1960), p. 139.

230. *EMZ,* 1960, p. 139.

231. *Zeitschrift für Religions- und Geistesgeschichte,* Cologne, X (April 1958), p. 335.

232. W. C. Lamott, *Revolution in Missions* (New York, 1954), p. 104.

233. *Missionsblatt Evang. Luth. Freikirchen,* LIV, 8 (1962), 150 (Bleckmar).

234. S. Schüller, *Geschichte der christlichen Kunst in China* (Berlin, 1940), pp. 10ff.

235. L. Frös, S. J., *Die Geschichte Japans* (Leipzig, 1926), pp. 465—68.

236. V. Cronin, *Der Jesuit als Mandarin* (1960?), p. 97; S. Schüller, pp. 37—39.

237. H. R. Williamson, *British Baptists in China 1845 to 1952* (London, 1957), p. 330.

238. Cronin, *A Pearl to India,* pp. 134, 146, 237.

239. *NZM,* XIII, 3 (1957), 236; K. Baer, *The Treasures of Mission Santa Ines, Fresno (Calif.), 1956;* idem, *Painting and Sculpture at Mission Santa Barbara, Washington 1955;* J. Butler, ibid., print on p. 13.

240. Ibid., p. 13; idem, "The Theology, etc.," ibid., p. 7; R. A. Klostermann, *Probleme der Ostkirche* (Göteborg, 1955), p. 189.

241. J. Specker, *Die Missionsmethode in Spanisch-Amerika im 16. Jahrhundert* (Schöneck-Beckenried, 1953), p. 195; M. Fassbinder, *Der "Jesuitenstaat" in Paraguay* (Halle [Saale]), 1926, p. 30.

242. *The Student World,* LII, 3 (1959), 303; *NZM,* XVII, 2 (1961), 88; H. Lilje, *Welt unter Gott* (Nürnberg, 1956), p. 54.

243. *Zeitschrift für Kirchengeschichte,* LXXII (1961), 99; *NCC Review,* LXXVIII, 2 (1958), 83f.

244. Butler, ibid., p. 2; *IRM,* XLVII, 187 (1958), 267; *Kunst und Kirche,* XXV, 2 (1962), 83, col. 1; *C. M. S. Outlook,* London (Aug. 1960), pp. 5, 12.

245. *L'Art Chrétien,* pp. 212f., 223—29.

246. *Katholisches Missionsjahrbuch der Schweiz,* 1962, p. 28; T. Ohm, pp. 695, 700ff.; 710—32; *EMZ,* 1957, pp. 43—44; *Ev. Miss.-Magazin,* 1956, pp. 98ff.

247. *Art and the Message of the Church* (Philadelphia, 1961), p. 130.

248. E. G. K. Hewat, *Vision and Achievement* (Edinburgh, 1960), p. 159; R. A. Felton, *Church Bells in Many Tongues* (Lebanon, Pa., 1958), p. 76.

249. J. W. Grant, *God's People in India* (London, 1960?), p. 38. Cf. *Kunst der jungen Kirchen,* pp. 51f., print 87.

250. R. Rutt, *The Church Serves Korea* (London, 1956), pp. 26, 38; D. Hyde, *Wem werden sie glauben?* (Freiburg, 1956), pp. 247, 276, 295; T. Ohm, *Kirchen und Kunst in Korea,* pp. 27—35.

251. C. Blumhardt, *Christus in der Welt* (Zurich, 1958), p. 218; H. and G. Taylor, *Hudson Taylor* (Thun, Switzerland), II, 70.

252. H. Lilje, *Welt unter Gott* (Nürnberg, 1956), p. 64; S. Holm, *Karl Ludwig Reichelt* (Oslo, 1952), pp. 16, 21, 23.

253. Nida, *Message and Mission,* p. 173.

254. Rev. R. J. Hammer to the author, March 3, 1959.

255. De Rover and J. Roessli, *Gottes Spur ist überall* (Constance, 1960), p. 201; *Gehet hinaus,* report on Austrian theological lectures, 1957 (mimeographed), p. 87; *Jahrbuch für Antike und Christentum* (Münster, 1958), p. 146; R. Christiansen, *For the Heart of Africa* (Minneapolis, 1956), p. 64.

256. A. Campell, *Afrika—Gesicht und Seele* (Stuttgart, 1954), pp. 345f.

257. *L'Artisan Liturgique,* X, 43 (Oct.—Dec. 1936), prints on pp. 890—91, 897, 904, 914—15, 917; *Liturgical Arts,* New York, XXII (Nov. 1, 1953), 17, 20—23; Costantini, *L'art Chrétien,* pp. 105—18.

258. *Scope of Total Architecture* (New York, 1955), pp. 16f., 95, 98.

259. The literature on building in the tropics is immense. John Butler presents a selection in footnote 10 of his contribution to the *Festschrift* to the author.

260. *Lutherische Rundschau,* Geneva, XI, 4 (1961), 273f.

261. *DWM News Letter,* Geneva, No. 9 (Oct. 9, 1958), p. 11.

262. *Katholisches Missionsjahrbuch der Schweiz,* 1962, pp. 78f.

263. "Entwurf für Neuguinea," *Kunst und Kirche,* XXV², (Feb. 1962), 86f.; cf. also pp. 81f.; *Plan und Modell für Ober-Volta, Afrika; Katholisches Missionsjahrbuch der Schweiz,* 1962, pp. 80—82; 2 prints in Butler, ibid., pp. 16f.

264. Lamott, *Revolution in Missions,* pp. 104f.

265. *Building Project of Yamato Christian Church* (Kyoto, 1959?); *Japan ruft,* Dec. 1959, p. 44.

266. Illustr. in De Rover and J. Roessli, after p. 224.

267. F. Kleemann, *Europäer und Asiaten* (Munich/Basel, 1957), p. 74; K. Goldammer, *Die Formenwelt des Religiösen* (Stuttgart, 1960), pp. 286ff.; A. Eckardt, "Wesen und Wirken der japanischen Malerei," *Universitas,* XIV, 3 (1959), 235—46; I. Sugimoto, *Tochter des Samurai* (Rowohlt, 1959), pp. 87f., 136; G. Rosenkranz, ed. *Christus kommt nach Japan* (Salzuflen, 1959), pp. 19, 84—87; J. Gonda, *Die Religionen Indiens, I* (Stuttgart, 1961), 338, 340f.; *World Mission,* New York, IV (Spring 1953), 14f.

268. *The Student World,* XLVIII, 2 (1955), 178; see bibliography in *EMZ,* 1960, p. 41; E. Tisserant, *Eastern Christianity in India* (London, 1957), p. 60; *IRM,* II, 204 (Oct. 1962), 432f.

269. Entries in the text from a letter of Missionary H. J. Becken to the author on Dec. 1, 1961.

270. *5000 Jahre Kunst aus Indien*, p. 40. Quoted in E. Schick, "Über die Begegnung zwischen Zen-Buddhismus und Christentum," *Evangelisches Missions-Magazin*, Basel, CII, 3 (1958), 121f.

271. Bahr, *Poiesis*, pp. 245ff., 290ff.

272. *Die Katholischen Missionen*, No. 4 (1959), p. 126; letters to the author dated March 4, 1959, and Dec. 5, 1958.

273. *Die Katholischen Missionen*, No. 4 (1959), p. 126, and No. 5 (1955), pp. 135—38.

274. Butler, ibid., . . ., p. 4, left col.; K. Goldammer, "Frühchristliche Kunst als Missionskunst," typescript for *Festschrift* to Arno Lehmann.

275. Elisofon, pp. 57f.; *Altertümer von Benin* appeared as a publication by the museum for ethnology, vols. IX and X (Berlin and Leipzig, 1919).

Index of Names

Index of Subjects

Picture Section

Africa   1–67

1. Sr. Ancilla, East Africa:
   Joseph and the Child Jesus

2. Rosemary Namuli, East Africa: *Burial*

4. Rosemary Namuli, East Africa: *Mary*

3. Lusi Namulondo, East Africa: *The Christ Child*

5. Avunilva, East Africa: *Battle Between the Shambala and the Masai*

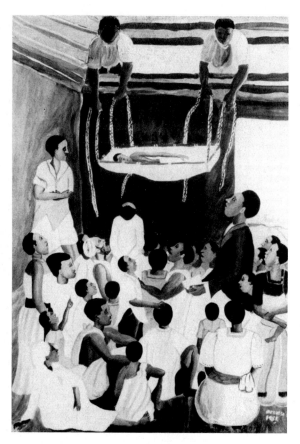

6. Napawesa, East Africa:
   Christ Heals the Paralytic

7. Elimo Philipp Njau, East Africa:
   The Baptism

8. Elimo Philipp Njau, East Africa: *The Crucifixion*

9. Sam J. Ntiro, East Africa: *The Nativity*

10. Sam J. Ntiro, East Africa: *The Entry into Jerusalem*

11. Charles Sekintu, East Africa: *The Resurrection*

12. Samuel Songo, East Africa: *The Resurrection*

13. Stephania Tunginie, East Africa: *The Temptation*

14. Sam J. Ntiro, East Africa: *The Crucifixion*

15. East Africa: *Mary and Martha*

16. East Africa: *The Flight to Egypt*

17. East Africa: *The Cursing of the Fig Tree*

18. East Africa: *Mary and the Child Jesus*

19. East Africa: *The Entry into Jerusalem*

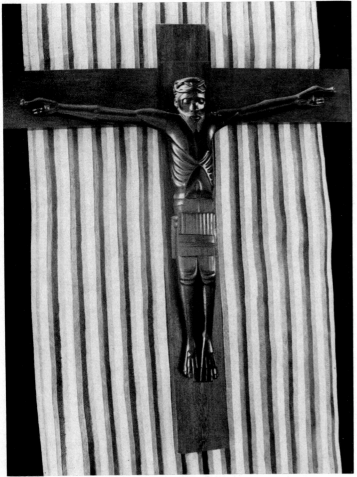

20. East Africa: *Crucifix*

21. East Africa: *Crucifix* (detail)

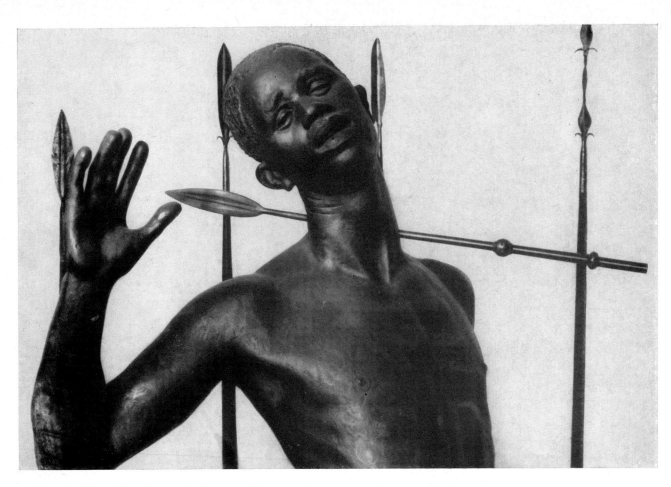

22. East Africa: *Statue of a Christian Martyr*

23. South Africa: *Adam and Eve*

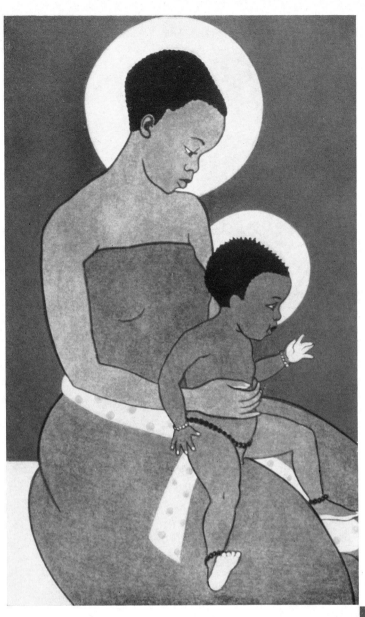

24. Rusi Beseriko, South Africa:
Mary and the Child Jesus

25. South Africa: *Crucifix*

26. South Africa: *Mary and the Child Jesus*

27. South Africa: *Dutch Reformed Church*

28, 29. South Africa: *Tombstones*

30. Justin Accobessi, West Africa: *The Flight to Egypt*

32. E. Addo-Osafo, West Africa:
Matthew 28:16-20

31. M. B. Adi-Dako,
West Africa:
2 Kings 23:1-3

33. M. B. Adi-Dako, West Africa:
Cover Design for St. John's Gospel

34. D. Agyei-Henaku, West Africa:
Matthew 28:16-20

IESU SE 'MONSA AYAREF
SƐ: ONYAƞKOPƆƞ AHEN

35. E.V. Asihene, West Africa: *Luke 10: 9*

YARE NA MUNSE WƆŊ
ABEŊ MO: Luk. 10. 9.

36. Cornelio and Gabriel,
West Africa:
The Promise to Abraham

37. Cornelio and Gabriel,
West Africa:
*Abraham on the Way
to the Place of Sacrifice*

38. Cornelio and Gabriel,
West Africa:
Job Under Tribulation

39. Cornelio and Gabriel,
West Africa:
Job After the Tribulation

IVI MAGDAL

40. Cornelio and Gabriel,
West Africa:
*Mary Magdalene Weeping
at the Sepulcher*

41. Cornelio and Gabriel,
West Africa:
*Mary Magdalene and Jesus
on Easter Morning*

42. Cornelio and Gabriel,
West Africa:
On the Road to Emmaus

43. Cornelio and Gabriel,
West Africa:
*Jesus Breaking Bread
at Emmaus*

44. Ben Enwonwu, West Africa:
    The Risen Christ

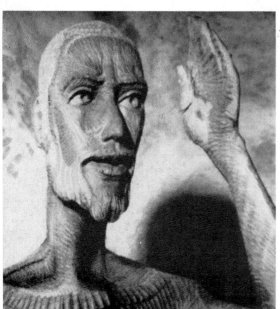

45. Ben Enwonwu, West Africa:
    The Risen Christ (detail)

46. Stephen Hountondji, West Africa: *The Temptation of Christ*

47. Michael Vodzgogbe, West Africa: *Greeting a Chieftain*

48. S. A. D. Lasekan, West Africa:
   Christ Blessing the Children

49. West Africa: *The Three Wise Men*

50. West Africa: *Mary and the Child Jesus*

51. West Africa: *Crucifix*

52. West Africa: *The Crucifixion*

53. West Africa: *St. Joseph*

54. West Africa: *St. Francis Preaching to the Birds*

55. West Africa: *University Chapel*

56. West Africa: *St. Peter's Lutheran Church in Monrovia*

57. Dupagne, Central Africa:
Mary and the Child Jesus (Congo)

58. Benjamin Mensah, Central Africa: *Slavery*

59. Central África: *Ecce Homo*

60. Africa (region unknown): *Mary and the Child Jesus*

61. Africa (region unknown):
Mary and the Child Jesus

62. Central Africa: *Altar*

63. Africa (region unknown): *Mary, Our Lady of Succor*

64. Central Africa:
The Eighth Station of the Cross

65. Africa (region unknown): *The Holy Family*

66. Fleming, Africa (region unknown): *Christ Carrying His Cross*

67. Africa: *Church at Adrar*

North America

68. Canada: *Mary and the Child Jesus*

69. Canada: *Mary and the Child Jesus*

70. Canada: *Crucifix*

71. Canada: *Crucifix*

72. Canada:
Crucifix

73. Richard West, U.S.A.: *Samson and Delilah*

74. Richard West, U.S.A.: *The Last Supper*

75. Richard West, U.S.A.: *Mary and the Child Jesus*

76. Richard West, U.S.A.: *Gethsemane*

77. Richard West, U.S.A.: *Gethsemane* (detail)

78. Richard West, U.S.A.: *Gethsemane*

79. Richard West, U.S.A.: *The Crucifixion*

80. Felipe, U.S.A.:
Christmas Dance

81. Felipe, U.S.A.:
Christmas Drama

82. U.S.A.: *Mary and the Child Jesus*

83. Hawaii: *Episcopal Church in Honolulu*

Central America

84. Castera Bazile, Haiti: *The Ascension*

85. Rigaud Benoit, Haiti: *The Nativity*

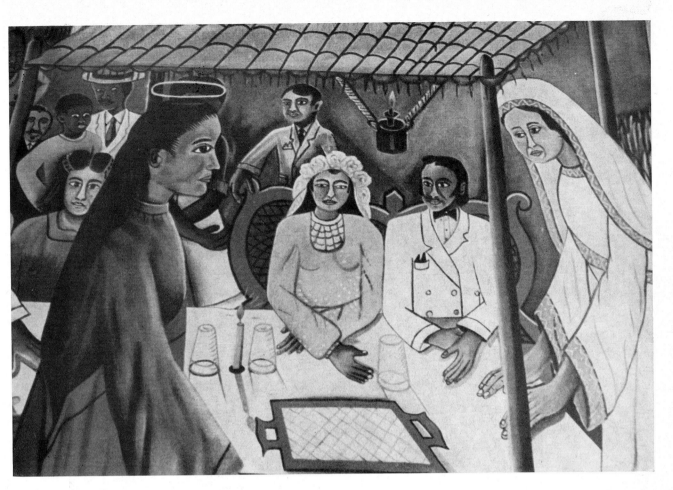

86. Wilson Bigaud, Haiti: *The Wedding at Cana* (detail)

87. Wilson Bigaud, Haiti: *The Wedding at Cana*

88. Philomé Obin, Haiti: *The Crucifixion*

89. R. Benoit, Ph. Obin, C. Bazile, G. Leveque, Haiti: *Mural*

90. Toussaint Auguste, Haiti: *The Nativity*

91. Castera Bazile, Haiti: *The Baptism of Christ*

92. Castera Bazile, Haiti: *The Cleansing of the Temple*

93. Jasmine Joseph, Haiti: *St. Peter*

94. Philomé Obin, Haiti:
    The Last Supper

95. José Quintero, Haiti:
    Mary and the Child Jesus

96. Mexico: *The Nativity*

Asia

97–236

97. Beyelel, Ceylon: *Mary and the Child Jesus*

98. W. De Silva, Ceylon:
The Miracle at Cana

99. W. De Silva, Ceylon:
*Christ on His Way
to Calvary*

100. W. De Silva, Ceylon:
The Burial of Christ

101. W. De Silva, Ceylon: *Descent of Christ from the Cross*

102. P. H. Wilson Peiris, Ceylon:
*Cathedral of Christ the King
at Kurunegala*

103. A. C. Canagarajah, Ceylon:
*St. Paul's Church
at Kilinochchi*

104. Ceylon: *Chapel*

105. Chang Chao-Ho, China: *The Flight to Egypt*

106. Mon van Genechten, China: *Guardian Angel*

107. Mon van Genechten, China:
The Crucifixion

108. Chang Chao-Ho, China: *The Sacrifice of Isaac*

109. Johnny Shek,
China:
Follow Me

110. Johnny Shek,
China:
Emmaus

111. Johnny Shek, China: *Matthew 26:14-16*

猶夫賣主

112. Johnny Shek, China: *Matthew 28:17-20*

113. Li-Ming-Yüan, China: *The Flight to Egypt*

114. Monika Liu Ho-Peh, China: *Mary and the Child Jesus*

115. Monika Liu Ho-Peh, China: *The Stilling of the Tempest*

116. Monika Liu Ho-Peh, China:
Peter About to Drown

117. Lu Hung-Nien, China:
The Mystery of the Holy Night

118. Lu Hung-Nien, China:
The Good Samaritan

119. Lu Hung-Nien, China: *The Annunciation*

120. Lukas Ch'en, China:
The Wise Men from the East

122. Lukas Ch'en, China:
Mary and the Child Jesus

121. Lu Hung-Nien, China:
*The Virgin Presenting the Child Jesus
to the World*

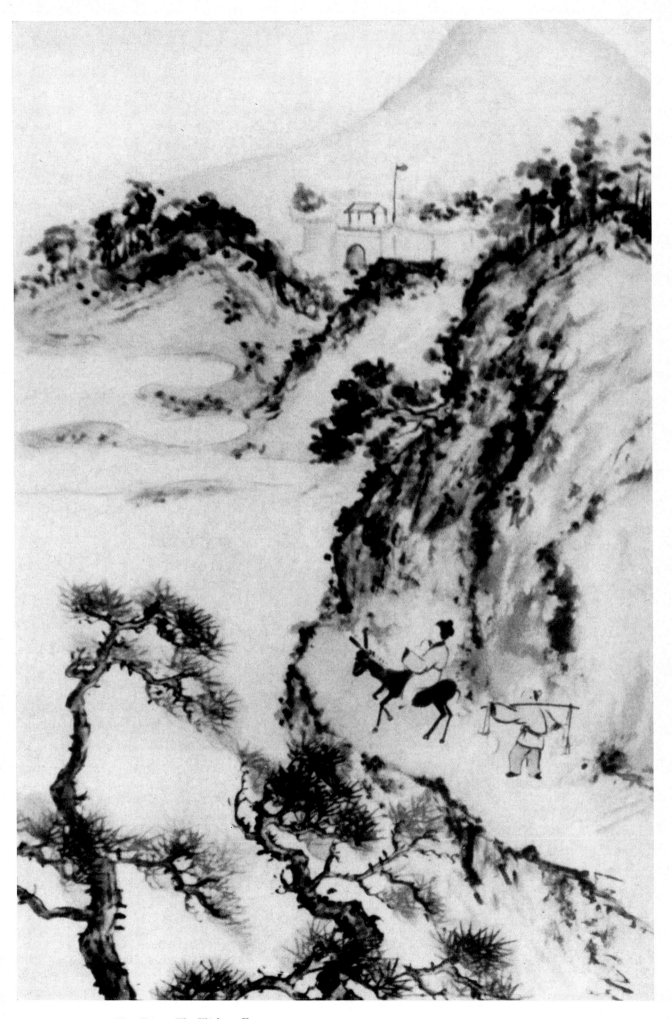

123. Tun-Jou-Ku, China: *The Flight to Egypt*

124. Tun-Jou-Ku, China: *The Heavenly Host*

125. Tun-Jou-Ku, China: *Mary and the Child Jesus*

126. Wang-Su-Ta, China: *Come, O Blessed of My Father*

127. Wang-Su-Ta, China: *The Flight to Egypt*

聖瑪利亞及耶穌
壽焉五翁遑敬繪廿...

128. China: *The Nativity*

129. China: *The Wise Men from the East*

130. China: *The Sower*

131. China: *The Lost Coin*

132. China: *St. Andrew's Church*

133. China: *Christ Church in Tao Fong Shan*

134. Chou I-Hung, China: *The Nativity*

135. I-Ching-Ku,
Hong Kong:
The Shepherds

136. I-Ching-Ku,
Hong Kong:
The Nativity

137. I-Ching-Ku,
Hong Kong:
*The Wise Men
from the East*

馬利亞已經選擇那上好的福分是不能奪去的
路加福音 第 十章 四十二

徐詠琴敬繪

138. I-Ching-Ku, Hong Kong: *Mary and Martha*

139. I-Ching-Ku, Hong Kong: *The Ten Virgins*

140. Hong Kong: *Martyrdom*

141. Hong Kong: *Lutheran Church*

142. S. S. Bundellu, India: *Matthew 24:40*

143. S. S. Bundellu, India: *Jesus and the Ten Lepers*

144. S. S. Bundellu, India: *Jesus and Judas*

145. S. Chavda, India: *Mark 15:22-24*

146. S. F. Carvalho, India: *The Flight to Egypt*

147. Arup Das, India: *Christ*

148. Arup Das, India: *The Last Supper*

149. Arup Das, India: *The Crucifixion*

150. Arup Das, India: *The Crucifixion*

151. Kanwal Krishna, India: *Christ*

152. Satish Gujral. India: *The Resurrection*

153. Devayani Krishna, India: *Christ*

154. S.Y.Malak, India:
Let the Children Come to Me

155. S.Y.Malak, India: *Luke 2:40*

157. S.Y. Malak, India:
Judas Bargains for Thirty Pieces of Silver

156. S.Y. Malak, India: *The Good Samaritan*

158. S.Y. Malak, India: *The Crucifixion*

159. S.Y.Malak, India:
Christ Appears to His Apostles

160. S.Y.Malak, India:
Ye are the Light of the World

161. V.S. Masoji, India: *Moses on Mt. Sinai*

162. V. S. Masoji, India: *Jesus Among the Teachers*

163. V. S. Masoji, India: *John 13:15*

164. V.S. Masoji, India: *The Return of the Prodigal Son*

165. V. S. Masoji, India: *The Raising of Lazarus*

166. V.S. Masoji, India: *The Savior on the Cross*

167. A. O. Pengal, India: *Healing* (Luke 8:43)

168. A.O. Pengal, India: *The Betrayal*

169. A.O. Pengal, India: *St. John*

170. A. O. Pengal, India: *Revelation*

171. Paul Raj, India: *Lord, Now Let Your Servant Depart in Peace*

172. Jehangir Sabavala, India: *Mary*

173. O. Rodrigues, India: *He Is Risen*

174. Jehangir Sabavala, India: *The Crucifixion*

175. Jehangir Sabavala, India: *Pietà*

176. Angela Trindade, India:
The Flight to Egypt

177. Angela Trindade,
India:
Luke 2:8-14

178. Angela Trindade,
India:
*Let the Children
Come to Me*

179. Angela Trindade,
India:
The Daughter of Jairus

180. Angela Trindade,
India:
Matthew 4:23

181. Angela Trindade,
India:
Mary and Martha

182. Frank Wesley, India:
The Nativity

183. Frank Wesley, India:
The Holy Family

184. India: *The Nativity*

185. India: *Christ and the Woman
at the Well*

186. Frank Wesley,
India:
The Madonna of the Lotus

187. Frank Wesley, India: *The Presentation in the Temple*

188. Frank Wesley, India: *The Pool of Bethesda*

189. Frank Wesley, India: *Jesus as a Boy in the Village*

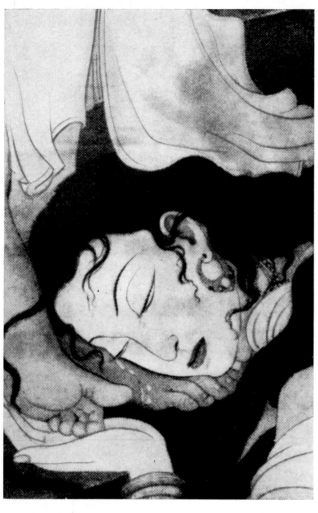

190. Frank Wesley, India: *Mary Magdalene Weeping at the Feet of Jesus* (detail)

191. India: *The Mother of God*

192. India: *Christ the Lord of all Nations*

193, 194. India: *St. Theresa's Church*
at Harigaon

195. India: *Christ Church*
at Rajahmundry

196. India: *Divine Service in Christ Church
at Rajahmundry*

197. India: *Window in Christ Church
at Rajahmundry*

198. India:
*Village Chapel
at Mandre*

199. India:
*Village Chapel
at Vakadi*

200. India:
*Cathedral
at Belgaum*

201. Indonesia: *Outdoor Pulpit at a Church Convention in Sumatra*

202. Wajan Turun, Indonesia: *The Nativity*
203. Wajan Turun, Indonesia: *Jesus Feeding the Multitude*

204. Wajan Turun, Indonesia: *Christ in Gethsemane*

205. Wajan Turun, Indonesia: *The Ascension*

206. Indonesia: *Mary and the Child Jesus*

207. Agha Behzad, Iran: *The Wise Men from the East*

208. Yoshikazu Kimura, Japan: *The Nativity*

209. Yoshikazu Kimura,
     Japan:
     Jesus and the Laborers

210. Yoshikazu Kimura,
     Japan: *Death*

211. Kimiko Koseki,
     Japan:
     The Test of Faith

212. Yoshikazu Kimura, Japan: *The Resurrection and Meeting with Thomas*

213. Yoshikazu Kimura, Japan: *Mary Magadalene*

214. Kimiko Koseki, Japan: *Japanese Martyrs*

215. Kimiko Koseki, Japan:
     Table Prayer

216. Sute Ota, Japan: *The Root of Jesse*

217. Sute Ota, Japan: *Eternal Life*

218. Japan: *Picture to Be Stepped On*

219. Sute Ota, Japan: *The Resurrection*

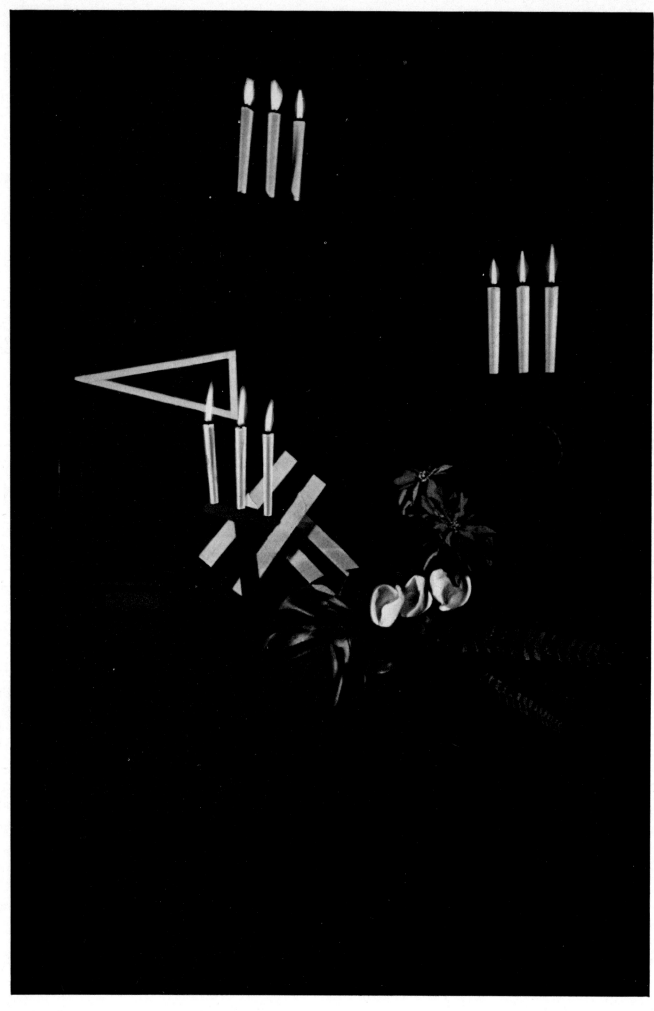

220. Sute Ota, Japan: *The Light Shines in the Darkness*

221. Sute Ota, Japan: *Labor Sunday*

222. Sute Ota, Japan:
Pentecost-Holy Spirit

223. Japan: *Mary and the Child Jesus*

224. Sute Ota, Japan: *Advent*

225. Sute Ota, Japan: *Christ the Light of the World*

226. Japan: *Mary and the Child Jesus*

227. Japan: *The Christ Child*

228. Japan: *The Birth of Jesus*

229. Japan: *Mary and the Child Jesus*

230. Japan:
*The Wise Men
from the East*

231. Japan:
*Lutheran Church
in Kamota*

232. Japan:
*Evangelical
Lutheran
Seminary Church*

233. Chang Woosung, Korea:
Christian Martyrs

234. Ki-Chang Kim, Korea: *The Nativity*

235. Lé van Dé, Vietnam: *Mary and the Child Jesus*

236. Taiwan: *Church*

Oceania

237. Dawidi, New Guinea: *Adoring Seraph*

238. Hesekiel, New Guinea: *Angel*

239. Hesekiel, New Guinea: *Wooden Baptismal Font*

240. Hiskia, New Guinea: *The Resurrection*

241. Qokomâc, New Guinea:
The Nativity

242. Qokomâc, New Guinea:
The Baptism of Christ

243. Qokomâc, New Guinea:
Gethsemane

244. Qokomâc, New Guinea:
The Arrest of Jesus

245. Qokomâc, New Guinea:
Christ on His Way to Calvary

246. Qokomâc, New Guinea:
The Crucifixion

247. Tine Kalai, New Guinea: *The Crucifixion*

248. New Guinea: *Crucifix*

249. Qokomâc, New Guinea: *The Gate of Heaven*

250. Qokomâc, New Guinea: *The Last Judgment*

251. Qokomâc, New Guinea: *The Resurrection*

252. Qokomâc, New Guinea: *Christ on the Rainbow*

253. New Guinea:
Group at the Crucifixion

254. New Guinea:
Crucifix

255. New Guinea: *Crucifix*

256. Hesekiel, New Guinea:
    Cain and Abel

257. Qokomâc, New Guinea: *Candelabra*

258. Reykepe and Mangkepe, New Guinea: *Two Figures of Christ and a Cross*

259. New Guinea: *Baptismal Crucifix*

260. New Guinea: *Crucifix*

261. New Guinea: *Baptismal Font*

262. New Guinea: *Wooden Baptismal Font*

263. New Guinea: *Crucifix*

264. New Guinea: *Crucifix*

265. New Guinea: *Wooden Baptismal Font*

266. New Guinea: *Baptismal Font* (detail)

267. New Guinea: *Lord, Abide with Us*

268. New Guinea: *Wooden Baptismal Font*

269. New Guinea: *Baptismal Shell with the Figure of Christ*

270. New Guinea: *Angel*

271. New Guinea: *The Altar in the Church at Ngasegalatu*

272. New Guinea: *The Church at Ngasegalatu*

273. New Guinea: *The Pulpit in the Church at Ngasegalatu*

274. New Guinea:
*The Baptismal Font
in the Church at Ngasegalatu*

275. New Guinea:
*A Column Supporting
the Church at Ngasegalatu*

276. New Guinea: *The Entrance to the Church at Ngasegalatu*

277. New Guinea: *Pulpit*

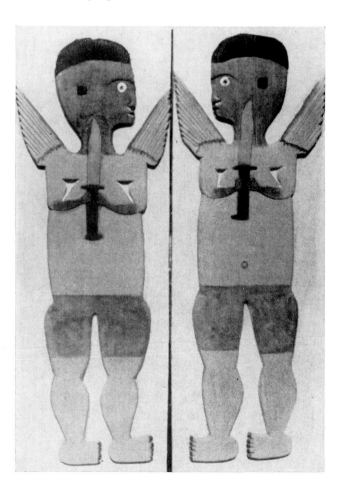

278. New Guinea: *Altar Painting at Gilang*

279. New Guinea: *Altar*

280. New Guinea: *Angel*

281. New Guinea: *Christ*

282. The South Seas: *Mary*

Appendix

List of Pictures with Comments

1. *Joseph and the Child Jesus*
By Sister *Ancilla*. Sr. Ancilla of Southern Rhodesia executed this work in clay (report in *Die Katholischen Missionen*, IV, 1959).

2. *Burial*
By *Rosemary Namuli* (print from *And Was Made Man*).

3. *The Christ Child*
By *Lusi Namulondo*, Uganda.

4. *Mary*
By *Rosemary Namuli*, a student in the Makerere College Art School (source same as print 2).

5. *Battle Between the Shambala and the Masai*
Painted by the Shambala man *Avunilva*, a Christian of East Africa.

6. *Christ Heals the Paralytic*
By *Napawesa* (source same as print 2).

7, 8. *The Baptism, The Crucifixion*
By *Elimo Philipp Njau* (source same as print 2). A letter dated Oct. 4, 1960, states that Mr. Njau was born Aug. 24, 1932, in Marangu of Kilimanjaro and teaches at the place where he received his education. In November 1960 he had his first "One Man Show," an exhibit of only his works. "My greatest desire is to serve God with my brush in Africa. I pray God that He may show His omniscience and omnipresence in Africa so that through Christ we Africans may gain self-confidence and have the courage and the strength to accept that which is *good* in the foreign, but to reject the many evil things and ideas that force their way into Africa."

9, 10. *The Nativity, The Entry into Jerusalem*
By *Sam J. Ntiro*, a Lutheran Chagga man. He was born April 20, 1923, in Machame, Tanzania, the son of a Kilimanjaro coffee plantation owner and oldest of eight children. In 1944 he went to study at Makerere College in Uganda and received his diploma in 1947. In 1952 he received a government Colonial Development and Welfare Fund Scholarship and studied until 1956 at the Slade School of Art and at the Institute of Education in London. Then in 1960 he traveled to the United States with his wife, Sarah Nyendowoha, who had studied at Oxford. He brought with him 60 of his paintings and sold them all, matching his sales at the Picadilly Gallery exhibit at the time when he was in London. Sam J. Ntiro, now professor at his former Makerere College, has done much painting and is one of the promising African artists. Under him also the Lutheran Chagga Christian, Elimo Philipp Njau (see prints 7, 8), attracted attention. His Christian paintings (in addition to a number depicting the life of the people and landscapes, for example, eucalyptus trees, village scenes, Chagga breweries, and others) constantly feature Africans. And so he places the Holy Supper into a round Chagga cottage.—In print 9 Sam J. Ntiro transfers the Nativity into a Chagga cottage. He sent the picture, characteristic of his painting, to his friends, saying: "As a Christian I am convinced that Christ must be one of us if Christianity is to penetrate our hearts."—On Sam J. Ntiro in *Oil Paintings on Life in East Africa* by Sam J. Ntiro, no date.

11. *The Resurrection*
By *Charles Sekintu* (source same as print 2).

12. *The Resurrection*
By *Samuel Songo* of Cyrene. The painting is in water-color and is displayed at Cuddesdon College in Oxford. The artist is crippled in both legs, and in the right hand only two fingers can be used for holding objects. The undamaged left hand is the working hand.—He has produced many paintings and sculptures. The chief school inspector of Matabeleland brought him to a Christian institution—as a hopeless case. Today Samuel Songo is favorably known in the world as artist, teacher, and also preacher in the school chapel (Arno Lehmann, *Die Kunst der Jungen Kirchen*, prints 33, 55).

13. *The Temptation*
By *Stephania Tunginie* (source same as print 2).

14. *The Crucifixion*
By *Sam J. Ntiro*. He has done a painting of the Anglican church of Kakindo (Uganda), which because of its architecture and furnishings became an "exciting pioneer venture." The artist himself said of the painting (1959): "Christ on the cross dominates in the composition through His size and His place in the painting. The seriousness of the great event is stressed by the dark colors of the Christ. Both the kneeling and the standing figures look at Him with sympathy and sadness on their faces. The inspiration for this painting came directly from my desire to express religious feelings in African forms of expression."

15. *Mary and Martha*
Children's art attracts attention and is exhibited throughout the world. India has annually a large Children's Competition and invites entries.

16. *The Flight to Egypt*
Abyssinian painting on canvas.

17. *The Cursing of the Fig Tree*
By a student of a girls high school in Gayaza (Uganda). Watercolor.

18. *Mary and the Child Jesus*
From Southern Rhodesia.

19. *The Entry into Jerusalem*
(Source same as print 2.)

20. *Crucifix*
This work of an African artist of the 20th century comes from the area of the Ndanda Abbey (East Africa).

21. *Crucifix* (detail)
A section of print 20. Elmer Jansen (Berlin) writes concerning it in the daily *Neue Zeit* of March 15, 1959: "The masklike, meaningful expression of this head of Christ grips us immediately. This is brought about above all by the material used: the ebony from which it is carved is hard, heavy, and deep black. We are startled especially by the unusual motif: Christ is represented as a Negro. The features are distinctly

African: stubby nose, high cheekbones, protruding lips, thick and somewhat curly hair. The traditions of native wood carving—the rigid, awe-inspiring forms of the totem poles—live in this representation. And yet something quite different is expressed here: Christ is drawn into this world of pictures and changes its standards of judgment. . . . The great hope is that the aspiring development of today in the black section of the world would lead to a blossoming of the arts. The ardent, searching look and the genuine confession of this head of Christ suggest an essential aspect of this blossoming. Attention is called to another Tanzanian wood carving of the crucifix, also from the present century, in Lothar Schreyer's *Christliche Kunst des XX. Jahrhunderts*, print 17, with text on pages 180—81 and 64, 148.

22. Statue of a Christian Martyr
The creator is unknown. It is only known that the Negro, D. Sebuggwao, was speared by his chieftain because of his faith and that later the chieftain and his tribe are said to have accepted the faith they persecuted.

23. Adam and Eve
Drawing by a student of St. Francis College, South Africa.

24. Mary and the Child Jesus
By *Rusi Beseriko*, Munyoro.

25. Crucifix
I have seen this crucifix in Holy Trinity Church in London, the headquarters of the Society for Promoting Christian Knowledge. At my request it was established that this is the work of an African in the U. M. C. A. Leper Hospital in Lindi of southern Tanzania. It is believed to have been done in 1955 or 1956. The name of the artist could not be learned.

26. Mary and the Child Jesus
The artist is unknown.

27. Dutch Reformed Church

28, 29. Tombstones
Cemetery of a Zulu congregation in Nazareth (Natal, S. Africa), 1939. Print 28: The tree of life is a symbol of the resurrection. Print 29: The tombstone was set up in 1932. The angel reminds of the angel that rolled away the stone from the tomb of Jesus.

30. The Flight to Egypt
By *Justin Accobessi*. A work in brass.

31. 2 Kings 23:1-3
By *M. B. Adi-Dako*, born 1927 and a member of the Presbyterian Church of Ghana; he is an "Art and Crafts Master" at St. Andrews Training College at Mampong (Ghana).—The text was proposed (among others) to Edinburgh for illustration in 1959. The drawing was made in March 1959.

32. Matthew 28:16-20
One of the proposed texts on which works were requested for the 1959 exhibit in Edinburgh.—The painter, *E. Addo-Osafo*, was 30 years old in 1958. He is a member of the Guan tribe, and his home is in Boso, Ghana. He describes himself as "a faithful and true member of the Presbyterian Church of Ghana."

33. Cover Design for St. John's Gospel
Drawing for the 1959 Edinburgh exhibit.

34. Matthew 28:16-20
D. Agyei-Henaku, a Ghanian, painted this picture for Edinburgh in 1959 and received a prize. He was born Dec. 29, 1928, and belongs to the Presbyterian Church of Ghana. He does not hide the fact that he has "only a half training in Art and Craft" and is not a "professional artist." He received his training as a teacher of drawing in 1953—1955 at the Kumasi College of Technology. He is now a zoological museum artist at the University College of Ghana in Legon (West Africa).

In addition to the prize and the recognition connected with it, Edinburgh brought him also a commission to paint. "I am waiting for the day when I receive the stipend so I can continue my training overseas."

35. Luke 10:9
By *E. V. Asihene*, teacher of drawing in a high school in Ghana. He is a member of the Presbyterian Church of Ghana and did this mural for the mission hospital of Agogo (1956).

36—43. The Promise to Abraham, Abraham on the Way to the Place of Sacrifice, Job Under Tribulation, Job After the Tribulation, Mary Magdalene Weeping at the Sepulcher, Mary Magdalene and Jesus on Easter Morning, On the Road to Emmaus, Jesus Breaking Bread at Emmaus
The wood carving appeared in 1960. They were done by two young wood-carvers, *Cornelio* and *Gabriel*, perhaps 20 years old. The pictures are placed in pairs one above the other (behind the main altar): the lower one expressing sadness, the upper one joy.

44, 45. The Risen Christ (45, detail)
By *Ben Enwonwu* (Nigeria). The work was carved from a mahagony block weighing four tons. It is in the chapel of the University College of Ibadan (Nigeria). "The artist gave the figure an extended body in conformity with his art and with the entire art of woodworking. The form of Mary (left) is naturally earthbound, for she wanted to prevent the risen Christ from leaving the world. The symbolical formation of the foliage behind Christ has received special praise from artists who have viewed the work." (Dr. James Welch, principal of the college)

46. The Temptation of Christ
By *Stephan Hountondji*. A work in brass.

47. Greeting a Chieftain
By *Michael Vodzgogbe* (Ghana). In his letters written at the time he made preparations to enter the 1959 Edinburgh exhibit he says he is "about thirty," that he belongs to the Ewe tribe, and is a Roman Catholic Christian.—The inspiration for this picture he received on a trip in 1957 to the Keta district. He painted the picture in 1958. It depicts a chieftain under a parasol signifying his dignity, surrounded by his leading men, and greeted by African women. The drums are "speaking drums."

48. Christ Blessing the Children
By *S. A. D. Lasekan*. Published as a postcard by the Society for Promoting Christian Knowledge, London.

49. *The Three Wise Men*
From Ondo (Nigeria).

50. *Mary and the Child Jesus*
From Oye-Ekiti, Nigeria.

51. *Crucifix*
From Angola. Before 1800.

52. *The Crucifixion*
From Dahomey, West Africa.

53. *St. Joseph*
From Nigeria. Wood decorated with paint.

54. *St. Francis Preaching to the Birds*
From Nigeria. Wood decorated with paint. (For a similar representation, also from Nigeria, see Rolf Italiaander, *Neue Kunst in Afrika*, print 28.)

55. *University Chapel*
Interconfessional Chapel of University College of Ibadan (Nigeria).

56. *St. Peter's Lutheran Church in Monrovia* (Liberia)

57. *Mary and the Child Jesus* (Congo)
By *Dupagne*.
   "O Mother of God and of our Negro world,
      you are black, you are nice."

58. *Slavery*
Also this picture from the Congo belongs to Christian art because the young sculptor, *Benjamin Mensah*, is a Christian.—"The theme of slavery is repeatedly treated with fondness by all African artists because they realized long ago that art adapts itself to ideological expressions." (Italiaander, *Neue Kunst in Afrika*, print 39)

59. *Ecce Homo*
Wood plastic.

60. *Mary and the Child Jesus*

61. *Mary and the Child Jesus*
Plastic of eucalyptus wood, height $12\frac{1}{2}$ in., 1959.

62. *Altar*
The Crucified is represented as a Negro, and all the objects on the altar are of African design.

63. *Mary, Our Lady of Succor*
Plastic of eucalyptus wood, height 5 ft., 1959.

64. *The Eighth Station of the Cross*
This station of the Way of the Cross was created in the studios of native art in Elisabethville in the Congo.

65. *The Holy Family*

66. *Christ Carrying His Cross*
A mural in the Roman Catholic Church of Tsumeb. The painter is a European, city planner *Fleming* of Windhoek, South-West Africa. The work appeared after World War II.

67. *Church at Adrar*
The church at Adrar in the Sahara belongs to the territory of the apostolic vicar of Ghardaia. Built entirely of red earth, it is in harmony with the style of construction in the land.

68—72. *Mary and the Child Jesus, Mary and the Child Jesus, Crucifix, Crucifix, Crucifix*

Eskimo works that appeared about 1962 in Povungnituk (northern Quebec).

73—79. *Samson and Delilah, The Last Supper, Mary and the Child Jesus, Gethsemane, Gethsemane* (detail), *Gethsemane, The Crucifixion*
These pictures were painted by an Indian, Prof. Richard West of Beacon College, Beacon, N.Y.

80. *Christmas Dance*
The Pueblo Indian *Felipe* in 1936—1941 painted 140 watercolors on the life of the Pueblos, who live on the Rio Grande in New Mexico. The abandoning of the tribal life that was to be hidden from the whites faced problems bordering on the magical. For that reason a pseudonym was used. Felipe attended a school and had perhaps some instruction in drawing, but his works show no American influence. It seems that he was a self-educated painter.—Among their many dances the Pueblos also had several Christmas dances, some in the church. The picture shows one of the dances performed in the open on the four days following Christmas. The picture made its appearance in June 1940. (E. C. Parsons, *Isleta Paintings*, p. 115)

81. *Christmas Drama*
By *Felipe*. After the dance in (!) the church and the midnight Mass the story of the birth was presented in the form of a drama. Women who had given birth in the past year and promised a shirt to the Child Jesus present the gift. All Indians kneel before the Child Jesus, pray, and smell the child (instead of kissing).—The picture was completed Jan. 6, 1941. (Parsons, *Isleta Paintings*, p. 113)

82. *Mary and the Child Jesus*
Indian applique and embroidery on woven background.

83. *Episcopal Church in Honolulu*
This Anglican church is the first church in Oriental architecture in Honolulu, Hawaii. (*Lambeth 1958 and You* [London: S.P.C.K., 1958], p. 13)

84. *The Ascension*
By *Castera Bazile*, 1950. This picture from "this fascinating and noteworthy Negro republic" (Bishop C. Alfred Voegeli) is one of the first paintings to make its appearance there. Music was there and was cultivated, but painting was unknown. The English teacher who found joy in painting, DeWitt Peters, brought with him in 1943 the first stimulus for founding an art center in Port-au-Prince.—Columbus came to Haiti in 1492. Under Spanish and French domination (from 1697) the native Indians were exploited and wiped out. Slaves were imported, and these "Negroes from proud and independent African tribes were treated with such degrading brutality that the entire working class had to be replaced every 20 years." The mixture of races that took place, creating the mulattoes, interpenetrated the populace. They are the forebears of the present-day elite Haitians. With them live the Negroes, who are Negroes insofar as they also are not a racial mixture. Into this world the Biblical event was brought and "interpreted." That explains the dark faces of the characters. Pictures 84—89 are murals that decorate the Holy Trinity Cathedral (Episcopal) in Port-au-Prince. After the founding of the art center in 1943

talents were discovered, "mostly persons who had learned to paint by themselves and whose work was in the true sense 'primitively' original." In 1948 Bishop Voegeli requested that the walls of Holy Trinity Cathedral be provided with paintings—this was to be the contribution of Haiti's Episcopal Church to the International Exhibition of 1949—1950 in Port-au-Prince. In the production of the murals nine painters participated. All except two belong to the "primitive school." On Haiti in general and on paintings see special Haiti number of *Forth*, 122 (New York, March 1957), No. 3.

85. *The Nativity*
By *Rigaud Benoit*, 1950, painted in the cheerfulness of colors typical of Negro art.

86, 87. *The Wedding at Cana* (86, detail)
By *Wilson Bigaud.*

88. *The Crucifixion*
By *Philomé Obin*, 1950.
The cross of the Redeemer stands on a residential street.

89. *Mural*
The apse of Holy Trinity Cathedral in Port-au-Prince. Three of the painters have already been mentioned (prints 84, 85, 88). The fourth, *Gabriel Leveque*, painted the angels in the upper part. Completed 1950 under supervision of Le Centre d'Art.

90. *The Nativity*
By *Toussaint Auguste.*

91, 92. *The Baptism of Christ, The Cleansing of the Temple*
By *Castera Bazile* (print 92 from 1951).

93. *St. Peter*
By *Jasmine Joseph.*

94. *The Last Supper*
By *Philomé Obin.*

95. *Mary and the Child Jesus*
Plaster of Paris relief of a black madonna by the Negro *José Quintero.*

96. *The Nativity*

97. *Mary and the Child Jesus*
This wood carving by *Beyelel* has appeared in our time. It is not free of Western influence, but it is not outright Western and does not leave that impression. Note the halo of the mother and the child with the strong rays of light.

98—101. *The Miracle at Cana, Christ on His Way to Calvary, The Burial of Christ, Descent of Christ from the Cross*
The painter of these pictures, Miss *W. De Silva*, a Ceylonese born May 28, 1935, is from a family of teachers and a member of the Methodist Church. Pictures 98, 99, and 101 are watercolors. The endeavor not to lose the historical background is unmistakable. In picture 100 the artist painted the preparation for the burial in oils (1957). It shows development and competence to work independently with strong lines and to bring native coloring into the picture.

102. *Cathedral of Christ the King at Kurunegala*
Architect *P. H. W. Peiris*, A.R.I.B.A., is Ceylonese and an Anglican Christian. He lives in Colombo. *The Ceylon Churchman*, 1960, pp. 131f., says: "The cruciform church is constructed in the authentic style of Ceylon." The high altar is built of local stone. The tower shows a distinctive Kandyan roof supporting a bronze cross. Inside on the east wall rises a statue of Christ above the altar and the bishop's throne, which faces west toward the congregation. It is the Christ of the Revelation of St. John, white with a golden crown and a pale-blue background. The statue was created by the Ceylonese artist *Issa Ranasinghe*, whose works have been bought in England by public and private collectors. At the feet of Christ is a high, stepped Cingalese brass stand for several oil lamps. Two simpler brass stands about as tall as a man serve the same purpose on the right and the left of the altar. The kneelers for receiving the Holy Sacrament of the Altar are in bright color familiar to the eye of a Ceylonese.—The cathedral was dedicated in the presence of about 1,300 Christians Jan. 21, 1960, by Bishop Dr. Lakdasa De Mel. At the beginning of the service he, the Lord Bishop of Kurunegala, asked the believers to kneel and to thank God in private prayer for the completion of the building and ask Him for His blessing, not forgetting to thank Him "for the beauty with which the architects, artists, and construction men have provided and decorated the house of God."

103. *St. Paul's Church at Kilinochchi*
This church in Dravidian architecture in northern Ceylon, whose members are mostly emigrant Tamils, is the only church of this style in all of Ceylon. It was dedicated Dec. 6, 1956. The architect is a Christian from the city of Jaffna. Also the builder of the church, V. Chinniah, is a Christian. A few government officials belong to the congregation and sometimes travel by car, but the majority of the members are peasants and laborers. The church and the parsonage, "Karuna Nilayam" (home of grace), are built entirely by funds given by the Tamilian and Cingalese Christians, the latter group contributing the major part. The ornamentation both outside and inside is in Dravidian style. The capitals of the columns each have four lotus flowers when the column is free-standing, but three and two respectively when attached to the wall. The interior reveals wide use of the banana motif. The lotus is a symbol of the purity of Christ, and the bunch of bananas of His resurrection (according to Chandran Devanesan in *The Student World*, 1955, No. 2, p. 178). A description with pictures of this church is in C. M. S. *Outlook* (London), Feb. 1958, pp. 2f.

104. *Chapel*
in the Training Colony of Peradeniya. This recent chapel is built in a different style, that of Central Ceylonese. The chapel serves a Christian teachers college as the place of worship. It has no doors or windows, thus taking the tropical climate into consideration in a special way.—There are also several other church buildings in Ceylonese style, such as the Church of Christ the Risen Lord, also in Peradeniya; Christ Church of Baddegama, and above all the Chapel of Trinity College in Kandy, which has been called "a

gem of Cingalese architecture" and in which the attempt to build "in the language of the land" has been successful. Print in Arno Lehmann, *Die Kunst der Jungen Kirchen*, p. 144, and the notes on p. 234. A good description with a plan and five prints was given by the principal of the college of that time, J. McLeod Campbell, in *A Cingalese Chapel for Trinity College, Kandy*.

105. *The Flight to Egypt*
By *Chang Chao-Ho*. Painted for the exhibition of Christian art in the Holy Year (1950) in Rome. "Chang was born 1904 in Luhsien in the Province of Szechwan. From early childhood he felt the urge to paint. Already as a boy he won renown in his home town with his drawings, and that without outside direction. At 16 he went to Shanghai, where he lived for a long time in abject poverty. His paintings soon attracted attention. He was called to the National University of Nanking and taught at the same time at the College of Fine Arts of Shanghai.—The art of Chang Chao-Ho is halfway between East and West. The Western influence is evident and deliberately intended. The Berlin painter Käthe Kollwitz influenced him strongly in style and the choice of themes. Like her, Chang loves to depict people in their need (*Weeping Mother Beside the Dead Body of Her Child*, and others). ... Despite this Western realism, which is so foreign to traditional Chinese art, he cannot hide the truly Chinese because of the traditional, highly expressive use of lines, which is related to Chinese calligraphy. This shows that also Chang paints his pictures in European style but 'writes' them in Chinese" (*Die Katholischen Missionen*, 1950, p. 148).—When Chang Chao-Ho painted these and other Christian themes, he was a non-Christian. This famous painter was engaged to illustrate the Chinese Bible translation of P. Allegra, O.F.M.

106, 107. *Guardian Angel, The Crucifixion*
By the Flemish artist-missionary *Mon van Genechten* who entered the Peking circle of artists in 1930. He became absorbed in Chinese art and culture so that he was able to resume under his Chinese name Fang Hsi-Sheng the lost artistic traditions of the great Jesuit artists of the 18th century. "Murals, wood carvings, landscapes, Christian paintings on silk made their appearance. He completely mastered the Chinese technique of painting, and his artistic ideas were inexhaustible. At times the Chinese did doubt his originality. But as they watched him at work, doubt gave way to real enthusiasm and genuine admiration." This man was no "strange devil from the West."—Mon van Genechten was born 1903 in Antwerp. Concerning this painter see *Die Katholischen Missionen*, 1950, pp. 42—47. By the painter himself: *Bij de Chinese Schilderijen*, no place, no date.

108. *The Sacrifice of Isaac*
By *Chang Chao-Ho*.

109—112. *Follow Me, Emmaus, Matthew 26:14-16, Matthew 28:17-20*
By *Johnny Shek* (Shek Kai-Nung), a young but highly productive and promising artist. He is an evangelical Christian. By him is also the original *The Flight to Egypt* in Arno Lehmann, *Die Kunst der Jungen Kirchen*,

print 107. Additional paintings by him are in *Sketches of Christ from a Chinese Brush* by Johnny Shek and Olaf K. Skinsnes (Minneapolis, 1956).

113. *The Flight to Egypt*
By *Li-Ming-Yüan*, a member of the painting instruction class of Lukas Ch'en. His photo is in Sepp Schüller's *Neue Christliche Malerei in China*, p. 49; a painting by him on p. 92; concerning him see p. 41.—"The water of the wide river is already wetting the feet of St. Joseph, and the donkey does not hesitate to follow him. How will the fleeing ones reach the other shore? Nowhere a house or a helper! The barren, knotty tree and the lower brush accent the impression of forsakenness. Seldom has the feeling of flight been depicted in such a gripping and striking manner as in this picture by the artist who always searched for a style of his own." (Ursula Graf)

114—116. *Mary and the Child Jesus, The Stilling of the Tempest, Peter About to Drown*
By *Monika Liu Ho-Peh*. In the silk painting (print 114) Mary wears the garment of a Chinese queen of ancient times. The top garment is red and the undergarment green, the decorations are stylistic mountains and ocean waves intended to symbolize regal dominion. The blue sash is a mark of authority, and the crown adorned with pearls and jewels is the symbol of sovereign majesty. Jesus is also fittingly clothed in the raiment of a king. He wears a yellow garment with a jade necklace and a medallion with the words "A Long Life" cut into it.—The artist was born 1928. The father and mother were respected professors of the natural sciences. The mother was an evangelical, the father a materialist. Monika was baptized as an adult. With her the mother, and lather also the father, became a member of the Roman Catholic Church. The painter sets forth her artistic and spiritual development in "I Paint for God," *Die Katholischen Missionen*, 1955, pp. 135—138.

117—119. *The Mystery of the Holy Night, The Good Samaritan, The Annunciation*
By *Lu Hung-Nien*, born 1914, leading student of Lukas Ch'en.—"In all my school years the drawing lessons were to me the most cherished. Already in my first year of attendance in the middle school I joined a study group for improvement in the art of painting. During my free time I practised drawing and painting continually. After passing the middle-school examinations I enrolled in the art department of the Catholic University. My father died the same year. At this time began my regular training in painting. In each of my three university years I ranked first, and in the final examinations I received the first prize of the art department."—Lu Hung-Nien as a non-Christian developed numerous Christian themes in painting. Whether he was baptized in the meanwhile remains unknown. According to Sepp Schüller, what inspired him in the Christian-Chinese painting was "the new influence of the Christian spirit on Chinese art, which had been cut off from the rest of the world through long centuries. The depth and forcefulness of expression in themes novel to the Eastern Asiatics led him through contacts with Lukas Ch'en to Christian subjects, which enabled him to become a leading artist of the new

Christian painting in China." (Arno Lehmann, *Die Kunst der Jungen Kirchen*, prints 103, 155, and notes on p. 234. Details concerning him in Sepp Schüller, *Neue Christliche Malerei in China* [Düsseldorf, 1940], pp. 36—41, 80, and prints on pp. 81—90.)

120. *The Wise Men from the East*
By *Lukas Ch'en*, the "Chinese Fra Angelico," known also as the painter of Mary, born 1901, baptized on Pentecost 1932. He is the originator of the new Christian Chinese painting and was professor of a class in painting at Fu-Jen University and at the first state school of art in Peking.—"Earlier, many Chinese artists despised and ridiculed me because I had accepted Baptism, which can be understood in the light of the conservative nature of the Chinese people. But I was not concerned about it. My work was different from that of others in two respects. For a time I painted ideas, Catholic ideas, altogether in the old Chinese style. For many that was something entirely new. Later many others varied their ideas all the way to the Chinese classicists, but without introducing new ideas. Their pictures were intended only to decorate the homes of the rich. My pictures had a different purpose: I wanted to be a courageous soldier of God . . . and if I should thus win friends for Chinese art in foreign countries, that would be a welcome result."—His picture, in which he is surrounded by leading students, is in Sepp Schüller, *Neue Christliche Malerei in China*, p. 49; concerning him, pp. 11—26, 51; paintings by him, pp. 52—64; also in Arno Lehmann, *Die Kunst der Jungen Kirchen*, prints 105, 108, 114, 124, 126, 174.

121. *The Virgin Presenting the Child Jesus to the World*
By *Lu Hung-Nien*.

122. *Mary and the Child Jesus*
By *Lukas Ch'en*.

123—125. *The Flight to Egypt, The Heavenly Host, Mary and the Child Jesus*
By *Tun-Jou-Ku*. On print 123: Similar and yet different from Johnny Shek's painting of *The Flight to Egypt* (Arno Lehmann, *Die Kunst der Jungen Kirchen*, print 107), Joseph carries the baggage in truly Chinese fashion on a carrying pole.

126, 127. *Come, O Blessed of My Father, The Flight to Egypt*
By *Wang-Su-Ta*, a Roman Catholic Christian born 1910, the son of a physician, baptized Christmas 1937, a leading pupil of Lukas Ch'en. On his life and work see Sepp Schüller, *Neue Christliche Malerei in China*, pp. 30—36, 72; see also Arno Lehmann, *Die Kunst der Jungen Kirchen*, prints 104, 111, 121, 123, 156, 173.

128—130. *The Nativity, The Wise Men from the East, The Sower*
From China.

131. *The Lost Coin*
The painting is a most felicitous "interpretation" of Luke 15.

132. *St. Andrew's Church*
This church was erected in the Wuchang industrial neighborhood to serve those employed in the factories. The year of construction is unknown, in any case before 1937. It was built by the Protestant Episcopal Church. Additional details in Daniel Johnson Fleming, *Heritage of Beauty*, p. 41.

133. *Christ Church in Tao Fong Shan*
This church was built 1934—1935 by the Chinese according to plans drawn by the Danish architect J. Prip Möller. It is a part of the Tao Fong Shan Christian Institute. To this "Mount of the Logos Wind" come thousands of Buddhist monks to lead a monastic life and to learn to know the faith of Christ. Many of them have desired to be baptized and have received Baptism. "The church and the entire arrangement are appealing to the eye because the architectonic forms of Buddhism, which fit into the landscape so well, have been utilized and given Christian form." Additional details in Sverre Holth, *Karl Ludwig Reichelt* (Oslo, 1952), pp. 16, 21, 23.

134. *The Nativity*
By *Chou I-Hung*. The picture was painted for use on a Christmas card and was printed in Switzerland in 1959.

135—139. *The Shepherds, The Nativity, The Wise Men from the East, Mary and Martha, The Ten Virgins*
By the painter *I-Ching-Ku*, who grew up in Wenchow. She was a teacher of painting and arranged three exhibits of her paintings. She created many posters, murals, and Christmas cards.—The three Christmas scenes are in watercolors, each one depicting an ancient symbol: the bamboo for peace, the pine for a long life, plum blossoms for the fivefold blessing.

140. *Martyrdom*
18th century (?).

141. *Lutheran Church*
Lutheran Diamond Hill Church built 1955.

142—144. *Matthew 24:40, Jesus and the Ten Lepers, Jesus and Judas*
By *S. S. Bundellu*, born April 14, 1922. "At the present time I am working as a teacher of drawing in a Scottish Mission College in Bombay, but my aim is to live as a free-lance Christian artist and treat only Biblical themes. My style of painting is Indian as well as semirealistic." He has received various awards, e. g., from the National Christian Council for his painting *The Lost Coin*; from Pope Pius XII he received a gold medal for the picture *The Ten Virgins* exhibited in Rome in 1950. "A first prize was awarded to me by the government of India for my poster on prohibition. I am the executive member of the India Art Society. I am connected with other art societies also, but my aim is to live as a Christian artist." (From a letter dated March 26, 1959)

145. *Mark 15:22—24*
By *S. Chavda*. Published in *Together* (December 1957), p. 41.

146. *The Flight to Egypt*
By *S. F. Carvalho*.

147—150. *Christ, The Last Supper, The Crucifixion, The Crucifixion*
By *Arup Das*, director of the Institute of Advertising and Visual Publicity in New Delhi. Born July 5, 1927. Arup Das is a Bengali and a Hindu and one of several

Hindus who have given attention also to Biblical themes.—On the "passion for Christian themes" among Hindu painters see "Chiaroscuro by A. S. R." in *Illustrated Weekly of India* (Aug. 5, 1962), p. 13.

151. *Christ*
By *Kanwal Krishna*, etching. From *Illustrated Weekly of India* (April 6, 1958), p. 12.

152. *The Resurrection*
By *Satish Gujral*. From *Illustrated Weekly of India* (April 17, 1960).

153. *Christ*
By *Devayani Krishna*, batik. From *Illustrated Weekly of India* (Nov. 15, 1959).

154—160. *Let the Children Come to Me, Luke 2:40, The Good Samaritan, Judas Bargains for Thirty Pieces of Silver, The Crucifixion, Christ Appears to His Apostles, Ye Are the Light of the World*
By *S. Y. Malak*, born July 15, 1899. He is a leading member of the Mehdi Bagh Institution founded by his father in 1892 for the purpose of serving moral improvement and religious enlightenment. His father held "that all religions are good and point the way toward the attainment of final perfection."—S. Y. Malak studied in the Sir J. J. School of Art in Bombay and received his diploma in 1934. He participates in the supervision of the Nagpur School of Art as well as in instruction and in the giving of examinations. He cultivates the Indian style without however adhering to a certain school or technique of painting. "Every tendency in style and every technique of painting are equally good insofar as they can be adapted by the artist to serve as a form of expression of his desire to serve and as an aid to its understanding." As he wrote Feb. 26, 1959, S. Y. Malak "painted pictures in oriental (Indian) as well as academic styles, using watercolour, oil, and pastels as medium. Though my favorite subjects are symbolical compositions I also paint portraits and other subjects." The second picture was done in 1954. Print 156, watercolor. Concerning his picture (print 157) he wrote: "This picture was painted in watercolors and follow the neo-Bengalese style, whose most famous exponent is Dr. A. N. Tagore. Three Brahmanic priests are in the picture (recognized by their cords) squatting on the ground at the temple entrance. They have set aside the things they will use in their cultic practices. The man standing asks the price for the betrayal, and with their fingers they indicate the number 30. Their crafty facial expressions are an indication of their insincerity. Such dark dealings prefer hidden places, and for that reason the dark shades of night were selected. Greediness and selfishness are indicated by the large stomachs."—The watercolor (print 159) shows the event recorded in Matt. 28:16-20: Christ appears to His disciples and sends them. "In this creation everything is typically Indian, the facial features as well as the clothing," explained Malak, and continued: "Our Lord is depicted in the traditional garb of His native country. This was done to place before the viewer the universal oneness of mankind in all the world. And to demonstrate that God's love and truth is for all, and to say it in an impressive manner, the apostles are represented as coming from

all vocations and social levels: as money lenders, Brahmanic priests, farmers, fishermen, etc." All have been called to follow Him and are to call others to Him also. Print 160: For the 1959 Edingburgh exhibit already mentioned in the text invitation was also extended to compete in the creation of a poster or cover design for the Gospel of John. The painter included with his painting an explanation: "Christ here stands on the terrestrial ball. He is clothed in a white 'dhoti' (sarong), symbolizing purity. The water-blue cloth over the upper part of the body has symbolical meaning: the poison of the world's sin has been made harmless. The peacock feather is to be understood as the antidote for a snake-bite, making the poison nontoxic. The red scarf worn as a turban expresses purity and love coupled with simplicity. The Bible, which contains the teaching of Christ, is bound in red, a color reminding of the life-blood of Jesus, who bore the sin of the world. The three strips of cloth at the end of the shepherd's staff remind of the Holy Trinity: white for God the Father, red for God the Son, and blue for God the Holy Spirit. These streamers on the staff are evidences of His authority to lead the wandering sheep (masses of humanity) that come to Christ, because He is the Light of the world. He shows them the right path as it is described in the Holy Word of God. And so they become the bearers of the light."

161—166. *Moses on Mt. Sinai, Jesus Among the Teachers, John 13:15, The Return of the Prodigal Son, The Raising of Lazarus, The Savior on the Cross*
By *Vinayak S. Masoji*, born Jan. 24, 1897, in Kolhapur. He is the son of a pastor and a member of the United Church of Northern India. His father was one of the few representatives of the young churches at the 1910 Edinburgh Conference. Masoji studies in Bombay and in Dr. Tagore's famous Santiniketan in Bengal. He also taught there for a few years and participated actively in ashram life. "Upon retirement in 1951 I became vice-principal of the Fine Arts Department (Kalabhavan)." His artistic activity, stimulated by extensive travel, included modeling in clay, leather work, wood-carving, etching, and batik work.—Concerning his picture (print 163) the artist wrote: "The mural *Jesus Washes the Disciples' Feet* was painted for the Christian Worker's Retreat Ashram at Alipore, a little village some 60 miles from Nagpur." The room is decorated with mango leaves (above the door), and incense is burned. These in addition to the flowers and the multilight lamp in the foreground make the scene festive and familiar to every Indian. Jesus smiles—Judas (at the right) with the left hand feels his purse and with the right hand seeks to prevent the act of the Master.

167—170. *Healing, The Betrayal, St. John, Revelation*
By *Albert O. Pengal*, a Kanarese and a member of the Methodist Church. Pengal was born Aug. 11, 1928, and lives in Bombay. He writes (letter dated July 25, 1959): "I am an amateur painter with a great interest in Biblical illustration."—Print 167 illustrates Luke 8:43.—The picture in print 169 was painted as a front-cover design for an edition of the Gospel of John. It was prepared for Edinburgh in 1959 and exhibited there. Christ is the Judge and the Savior of the world.

269

His grace belongs also to the adulteress "caught in the very act of adultery," as well as everybody else. The background for everything is the cross, with the Cruci-fied stretching out His Savior arms. The picture is an illustration of John 8:4-11.

171. *Lord, Now Let Your Servant Depart in Peace*
Watercolor by *Paul Raj*. From *Der Große Entschluß* (December 1952), following p. 72.

172. *Mary*
By *Jehangir Sabavala*, born 1922 in Bombay, where he still lives. Sabavala calls himself "a Parsi, Zoroastrian." He studied in Bombay and London and spent a few years in Paris. He received the Grand Prix de Peinture de Monte Carlo, exhibited in the Salon National Indé-pendent in Paris, and had many successful exhibitions in Bombay, Basle, Vienna, and New Delhi. He is one of the topnotch Indian painters of today. His palette is "always vibrant" because he is constantly experi-menting with new possibilities of expression. Even the Adelaide Museum of Australia has purchased works of Sabavala.—The painter calls the picture *The Madonna of the Holy Ghost*, painted in 1958.

173. *He Is Risen*
By *O. Rodriques*. From *Together* (December 1957), p. 42.

174, 175. *The Crucifixion, Pietà*
By *Jehangir Sabavala*. The picture (print 174) appeared in the *Illustrated Weekly of India* April 17, 1960. The weekly continues to publish specimens of new Christian art.

176—181. *The Flight to Egypt, Luke 2:8-14, Let the Children Come to Me, The Daughter of Jairus, Matthew 4:23, Mary and Martha*
By *Angela Trindade*, a Catholic.

182, 183. *The Nativity, The Holy Family*
By *Frank Wesley*, a well-known and cherished Indian painter, whose forebears were Mohammedans and Hin-dus. He is fourth generation North Indian Christian.

184. *The Nativity*
From India.

185. *Christ and the Woman at the Well*
From India. The picture is from 1941.

186—190. *The Madonna of the Lotus, The Presentation in the Temple, The Pool of Bethesda, Jesus as a Boy in the Village, Mary Magdalene Weeping at the Feet of Jesus*
By *Frank Wesley*. Print 190 is a detail.

191. *The Mother of God*
Unknown artist. Bronze. The figures stand on a lotus. Everything follows the Hindu form of art as it is best known in the representations of Siva Nataraja (for example, Hermann Goetz, *Indien. Fünf Jahrtausende indischer Kunst* (Baden-Baden: Holle Verlag, 1960²), pp. 187, 189, also 147).

192. *Christ the Lord of All Nations*
Christ on a lotus in the lotus posture of a Christian teacher. The right-hand fingers present an inviting gesture. The peoples are represented by their mothers. The picture is from 1939.

193, 194. *St. Theresa's Church at Harigaon*
Oct. 3, 1950, the plans, drawn by a German architect, were before those who were ready to build. The Catho-lic Christians themselves broke ground for the founda-tion. "The construction is simple: reinforced concrete pillars connected by thin walls. Cement blocks were used as construction material. ... The surface of the blocks is of a coarse mixture, giving the blocks a grain similar to that of natural stone. ... The construction costs—estimated at 50,000 Rs = $ 10,000—were de-frayed by collections among our Harigaon Christians, who are the poorest of the poor in India. Catholics from Poona and Bombay also brought contributions," but the larger part came from overseas.—A letter from one of the missionaries who had the church built states: "St. Theresa's Church in Harigaon is not of course the first church in India to be built in Indian style, but it is a bold experiment because it is the first church in India where an attempt was made not only to copy an old Indian style but to build it in modern Indian style and thus create something new. The attempt was made to fashion a church that is Christian in spirit, Indian in tradition, and modern in style. In other words, in coming to the church it should be apparent that this is a church and not an Indian temple, that this church was built in India and not in Europe, and that it was built in the 20th century."

195—197. *Christ Church at Rajahmundry, Divine Service in Christ Church at Rajahmundry, Window in Christ Church at Rajahmundry*
Print 195: This is the chapel, the "Luthergiri Chapel," of Lutheran Theological College at Rajahmundry, dedicated March 18, 1960. The tower over the chancel "is designed from the peculiar Indian gopuram which marks almost every Indian temple," but something new has taken place. The crosses in the tower are visible miles away.—Print 196: Mats instead of seats provide more sitting space and conform with the Indian way of sitting. Twelve beautifully decorated electric lamps were endowed during the time of construction in the fall of 1959.—Print 197: The main symbol in each window is the climbing vine of John 15:5: "I am the vine, you are the branches." The outstanding feature in each window both on the left and on the right are the seven large symbols: the hand of God, the Deca-logue, the Bible, the Lamb of God, the dove (for the Holy Spirit), the lotus as a symbol of India (print 197), and the cross on top of the globe. The balcony, which provides room for 100 people, also has the climbing-vine motif, as may be seen from print 196, which also appears in the chancel windows. The "individual motif" of the left window depicts the torch of wisdom, the right window a staff entwined with a serpent as a reminder that Christ is the great Healer who taught and healed and that His church is to be not only a teaching but also a healing church.—All material for the flooring, the lec-tern, the baptismal font, and the altar is either native stone or beautiful rosewood. Description in "The Luther-giri Chapel Christ Church, Lutheran Theological College, Dedicated March 18, 1960," Rajahmundry 1960; also in *The Foreign Missionary*, June 1960, pp. 16—17.

198. *Village Chapel at Mandre*
Roman Catholic.

199. *Village Chapel at Vakadi*
Catholic Christ the King Chapel.

200. *Cathedral at Belgaum*
Imitation of Moorish style is unmistakable in the construction of this Catholic cathedral.

201. *Outdoor Pulpit at a Church Convention in Sumatra*
The East Asia Christian Conference was opened March 17, 1957, in Liberty Square (an open area) in the city of Pematangsiantar with a "mammoth church day." Before 9 o'clock 100,000 people had gathered at the site. President Dr. Ahmed Sukarno came there from Djakarta by plane with a large civil and military escort. He spoke at the gathering and again in the afternoon at a reception he gave for the delegates. On this occasion also the Minister of the Interior, a Mohammedan, spoke. He stressed the principle of religious liberty in Indonesia, stating also that the Christian religion cannot be considered a foreign, imported religion, for it had its origin in Asia and therefore has a place and a task to carry out in the national life of Asia (*The Common Evangelistic Task of the Churches in East Asia* [Prapat, 1957], pp. 9 ff.). The appearance of the free-standing pulpit reminds ot the Malay style of building houses.

202—205. *The Nativity, Jesus Feeding the Multitude, Christ in Gethsemane, The Ascension*
These pictures from Bali were featured already in the *Zendingskalender 1959* (Zendingsbureau van de Nederlands Hervormde Kerk in Oegsgeest).—The painter is a young Balinese, *Wajan Turun.* To my knowledge he is not a Christian, certainly not when he painted the pictures presented here and many others with Christian themes. The report I received earlier that "almost nothing so far" is extant in the area of national art (Arno Lehmann, *Die Kunst der Jungen Kirchen*, p. 20) has been confirmed in recent correspondence, calling attention to the entirely different situation in the field of music and architecture. The "almost nothing in the area of national art" applies to the Christians of Indonesia. Wajan Turun is most productive. As Prof. Dr. Th. Müller-Krüger wrote me Sept. 17, 1962, he discovered on a visit to Turun's village in Ubud of Bali that a large group of heathen Balinese painters were following his example and selecting Biblical themes because they found a brisk market for them among the American tourists. I am indebted to Rev. F. L. Cooley of Djarkata for the information that he gave Wajan Turun, whom he knows well, the assignment to paint what he found and saw in four Bible passages. Thus appeared also the picture *Christ in Gethsemane* (print 204). But that was not the end of it: Wajan Turun has painted many Biblical pictures. As has been held, his style of painting corresponds with the Balinese tradition, but the color technique was learned from European artists, especially from the Dutch painter Bonnet, who was in Bali for a decade.—Criticism of Turun's paintings has already been expressed in the text. The fact seems to be that the Indonesian Christians and their leading men reject this type of native art. His paintings "seem to prefer Christian art in non-Indonesian form, either the Palestinian or the European." My correspondent from Djakarta, however, takes into consideration the facts that the adverse attitude toward Indonesian style of art will gradually give way to a new understanding already encountered with joy in the field of music.—Also Lukas Ch'en began as a non-Christian to paint Christian pictures and had a class in painting with gifted students. We also stand at the beginning and rejoice over what the future may bring. It cannot be denied that in these paintings much that is good has been "translated" into Balinese.—On print 204: What was said about the picture *Gethsemane* by Lukas Ch'en applies here: "His Christ is no deeply disturbed Christ in agony. He is the Jesus in forsaken quietness and deep peace. This interpretation is truly Chinese (in this case Hindu), but does not measure up to the Biblical text at the crucial points, and so the picture needs correction." This will take place, as in the presentation of the prodigal son. Also there the Bible came through, and people gave ear. "Such an example should serve us as a welcome reminder that we should be patient and that we must help our friends and allow them time for development. This we may do in the certainty that with inner growth the painter will submit to the Bible and muster the necessary courage to break through the obstacles of custom and tradition in order to respect the statements of the Bible (*Evangelische Missionszeitschrift* [1960], p. 42; Arno Lehmann, *Die Kunst der Jungen Kirchen*, p. 35).

206. *Mary and the Child Jesus*
From Bali

207. *The Wise Men from the East*
By *Agha Behzad*, an Iranian Christian. His wise men are members of the learned priestly class of ancient Persia. The picture appeared in 1958 as a World Christian Art Christmas card. (*World Literacy and Christian Literature*, New York)

208—210. *The Nativity, Jesus and the Laborers, Death*
By *Yoshikazu Kimura*, a Japanese pastor.

211. *The Test of Faith*
By Maria Theresia *Kimiko Koseki* (see notes on prints 214, 215).—A cutout from a silk screen *A Sumurai Family Faces the Decision*. Only one step, a brief treading on the "holy picture" (Fumi-e, print 218), and the parents and five daughters and the infant would be allowed to live—or face a torturous martyrdom. "Every one who acknowledges Me before men, I also will acknowledge before My Father who is in heaven; but whoever denies Me before men, I also will deny before My Father who is in heaven" (Matt. 10:32-33).—What a struggle especially for the two young girls at the right. It is necessary to meditate at length on this picture and let it speak to oneself. The Lutheran Church teaches in Article XXI of the Augsburg Confession that we should recall to mind the saints for the strengthening of our faith ... and so we would take their good works as an example for ourselves. Cf. notes on prints 214, 218.

212, 213. *The Resurrection and Meeting with Thomas, Mary Magdalene*
By *Yoshikazu Kimura*

214, 215. *Japanese Martyrs, Table Prayer*
By *Kimiko Koseki.* "My thoughts were bent toward art from my childhood. After completing the Girls Middle School I moved with Mother to Tokyo and attended

the Art Academy for four years. After the death of my mother I became a student of the famous master, K. Kawaseki. This master observed the special qualities of his students and urged them toward self-development. ... I became a Catholic in 1923 while still a student at the Art Academy. A friend pointed the way in time of my heartfelt need ... I felt the emptiness of life. I yearned for religion, and the friend showed me the direct route. Since the founding of the Catholic artists group I have applied myself to religious art. The hope glimmers in my soul that I may be permitted to praise my God with my colors. For all the good that He has given me since my baptism I hope to thank Him with my art."—Concerning the artist see Sepp Schüller, *Neue christliche Malerei in Japan* (Freiburg, 1939), pp. 76 ff.—On print 214: Already at an early date cruel persecution of Christians took place in Japan. A prayer is extant from April 8, 1603, a prayer of repentance for Christians who where overcome by the temptation to deny their faith. Tens of thousands of Japanese lost their lives as confessors of their faith; they were burned, crucified, hanged. ... A "very simple" way was offered for saving one's life. It was not necessary to deny with the mouth. It was necessary only to step on a "holy picture" (Fumi-e, see notes to prints 211, 218). One was thereby saved and again a Buddhist. The Fumi-e is before them. It was either denial or faithfulness and perserverance in the faith. (See Arno Lehmann, *Die Kunst der Jungen Kirchen*, prints 130—133.)

216, 217. *The Root of Jesse, Eternal Life*
By *Sute Ota* (see note on print 219).

218. *Picture to Be Stepped On*
At the time when secret Christians were hunted and persecuted a "holy picture" (Fumi-e), usually wrought in bronze, was mounted on a wooden base. Prints are included in *Namban Art* under the numbers 13 (Christ), 32 (Mary and the Child), 136—139 (The Madonna), 140 (Jesus Taken Down from the Cross), 146 (The Bound Christ, The Crucified, Jesus Coming Down from the Cross, The Madonna and the Child), 151—153 (oils on copper plates, used as Fumi-e).

219—222. *The Resurrection, The Light Shines in the Darkness, Labor Sunday, Pentecost-Holy Spirit*
These pictures were created by Mrs. *Sute Ota* (see also prints 216, 217). Flower arrangement is a fine art in Japan. The series of pictures appeared recently. They are based on the art of flower arrangement and thus convey a spiritual message (see also prints 224, 225).

223. *Mary and the Child Jesus*
A painting on silk.

224, 225. *Advent, Christ, the Light of the World*
By *Sute Ota*.

226—230. *Mary and the Child Jesus, The Christ Child, The Birth of Jesus, Mary and the Child Jesus, The Wise Men from the East*
From Japan. Print 227 is a Christmas card.

231. *Lutheran Church in Kamota*
Dedicated April 30, 1958. Size, 45 × 30 ft. Seating capacity, 120.

232. *Evangelical Lutheran Seminary Church*
Dedicated March 1, 1958. Size, 65 × 30 ft. Seating capacity, 140.

233. *Christian Martyrs*
By *Chang Woosung*.

234. *The Nativity*
By *Ki-Chang Kim*.

235. *Mary and the Child Jesus*
By an Annamese painter *Lé van Dé*.

236. *Church*
An example of the new will to build also in Taiwan.

237. *Adoring Seraph*
Carved by *Dawidi* according to Isaiah 6:2. Papua church in Ngasegalatu.

238, 239. *Angel, Wooden Baptismal Font*
Artist *Hesekiel*, about 50 years of age, is a teacher and an evangelist. He carved the baptismal font in 1958 for the church in Sio.

240. *The Resurrection*
By *Hiskia*, a pastor in Sio. A carving from hardwood. The two figures at the sides represent disciples.

241—246. *The Nativity, The Baptism of Christ, Gethsemane, The Arrest of Jesus, Christ on His Way to Calvary, The Crucifixion*
These pictures and carvings were all created for the church in Kotna by Qokomâc, an old teacher and evangelist from Sattelberg who spent his entire life working in Ogelbeng and Kotna. His paintings and sculptures are all in the Hagen area.—Print 242: Crayon on wood. Print 243: Instead of the conventional cup the angel presents the cross. In the background the disciples; Jesus with the crown of thorns at the left. Print 244: Black and white oil color on wood. Left: Jesus taken captive. Right: Jesus before Pilate. Print 245: Oil color on wood. Print 246: Oil and crayon on wood.

247. *The Crucifixion*
By *Tine Kalai*. Carved in 1927 from hardwood. Kalai comes from the village of Sialum on the eastern coast of New Guinea, 40 miles north of Finschhafen. The total height of the three carvings is 26 inches; the figure of Christ alone is 17 inches in length. In the Neuendettelsau Mission Museum since 1930.—The following is from the diary of Missionary Wacke concerning the mission station at Sialum-Kalasa (n. d.): "The natives themselves were to carve a decoration for the altar in the form of a crucifix. Both the Sialumese, living on the coast, and the inland people were to make an attempt. In the inland it was Kalai, and Tawak on the coast. It became evident that Kalai had the eye and the imagination of an artist. In speaking with him I detected that with his inner eye he saw in the trunk of the tree a picture of what he wanted to create. Tawak on the other hand leaned too heavily on ancient ancestral pictures. Kalai's work was definitely superior and was chosen as the one to be exhibited. When a photograph arrived at the office of the organization collecting items for the promotion of religious knowledge at Marburg, an order was placed for a like crucifix for the Marburg collection. ... When the question arose why Tawak did not succeed in creating a crucifix, Kalai explained: 'For such

work one must be alone with God, far away from the village, and speak very much with Him.' And so he always did his work far away from the village or thoroughfare in an out-of-the-way wilderness hut."—D. Georg Philhofer added the information (Sept. 27, 1962) that perhaps Kalai was a member of the Ono tribe and therefore belonged to the large Kate tribal group. It should be added that Tine Kalai used only the simplest tools: a hatchet, a cutting instrument with a handle used on the knees, a large knife, and a pocket-knife.

248. Crucifix
From New Guinea.

249—251. The Gate of Heaven, The Last Judgment, The Resurrection
By *Qokomâc*, likewise created for the church at Kotna (see prints 241—246). Print 249: Oil painting on wood. Print 250: Oil painting on veneer. Plate 251: The guards in the foreground, the angel in the background.

252. Christ on the Rainbow
By *Qokomâc*. The picture is in the church at Poklabena Ogelbeng. The figure stands out from the carved wood block in relief. The main lines in chip carving are painted with oil colors.

253. Group at the Crucifixion
The group at the crucifixion (height, 20 inches) is on the altar of the church at Sio on the northern tip of New Guinea. The entire creation is of ironwood, an extremely hard wood. It appeared about 1950 and is now in the possession of Dean Schwinn in Feucht-wangen. Prof. Dr. Georg Vicedom wrote concerning it: "The disproportionate arrangement of the group stands out. While the figure of Christ covers the entire cross, the other figures have been kept small. It is not clear whether the artist had in mind the two malefactors or Mary and John. The fact that both figures are men speaks against the latter assumption. The Crucified is also unsymmetrical. The disproportionately long body rests on short, stocky feet. The length of the arms must have fitted the dimensions of the wood. For that reason the artist's difficulty with the hands is notice-able. The face of the Crucified has Papuan features. The most original aspect in the group is the bird on the cross. It is not the bird of death waiting for its prey, but is supposed to be a dove, the symbol of the Holy Spirit. The bird is proof that the artist was troubled about the suffering of Christ. He could not conceive how the Lord Jesus could bear the terrible pains without the comfort of the Holy Spirit. This thought has found no expression in Western art."—Prof. D. Walter Freytag pointed out the following on Pente-cost 1959: "When the Papuans of New Guinea began to furnish their first self-constructed church with their own carvings, unusual things were to be seen. Figures of the apostles appeared that were clearly developed from the representations of man as found in the tradi-tional ancestor poles and as these foreshadowed the mystery of the beginnings which give life to all existence. Beside them are angel figures in ponderous form in crude colors, lacking all loveliness and sweetness, evidently God's messengers, enveloped in brightness, severity, and compassion, in what may be called

visitation. Representations of the Holy Spirit are almost as frequent as those of the cross. Very often one could see a cross, on the top of which was perched a dove in peaceful pose. Of this we have no Western examples. None of the missionaries could give infor-mation as to how the Papuans may have hit upon such a combination. I therefore asked an old man who knew of blood feuds and cannibalism from personal experience what the combination of the cross and the dove meant. He was not a little surprised at my lack of imagination. 'Don't you have eyes?' he asked. Then he continued, 'We have seen God and His power. That is our joy.' 'Seen God'—and with that he pointed to the cross on which He whom we have forgotten loved us unto death. And His power—that was the dove, the Spirit, the seal of His presence, the Spirit through which He comes to us also, receives us, calls us, and does His work among us. 'That is our joy.' ... The Holy Spirit was to this simple man of the Southern Seas the reality of God who despite all human realities is among us and in us, also despite the reality of the church, and continues His work." (From *Ökumenische Rundschau*, 10 [April 1960], 57. Reprint in Walter Freytag, *Reden und Auf-sätze* [München, 1961], I, 150.)

254, 255. Crucifixes
From New Guinea.

256. Cain and Abel
By *Hesekiel*, carved in 1958 for the church in Sio.

257. Candelabra
By *Qokomâc*, carved from a block with primitive tools. They are about 44 inches high and are in the church at Kotna. The angel in the middle has a beard because "Hagen people always have a beard, and so that is their conception of the angels" (Missionary Jäschke).

258. Two Figures of Christ and a Cross
Reykepe (left) and *Mangkepe* carved these figures sometime after 1945 for the new church at Domut. This art sprang from their hearts. The works present Christ, from whom the rays of love and glory go forth. (For this information I am indebted to H. Wagner.)

259, 260. Baptismal Crucifix, Crucifix
From New Guinea.

261. Baptismal Font
Gawaing, Sattelberg (New Guinea). A reference to Romans 6:3: "Do you not know that all of us who have been baptized into Christ Jesus were baptized into His death?"

262. Wooden Baptismal Font
Tipsit (Komba area)

263, 264. Crucifixes
From New Guinea.

265. Wooden Baptismal Font
Komba (New Guinea).

266. Baptismal Font
Detail of print 261.

267. Lord, Abide with Us
A figure from the Wantot area at the foot of the Finisterre Mountains, bearing the above inscription.—A blessing on the way.

268. *Wooden Baptismal Font*
Tehanuwe (New Guinea), 1960.

269. *Baptismal Shell with the Figure of Christ*
Hengure church (Timbe), Ulap (New Guinea).

270. *Angel*
Wood carving from Zaka (New Guinea).

271—276. *The Altar in the Church at Ngasegalatu, The Church at Ngasegalatu, The Pulpit in the Church at Ngasegalatu, The Baptismal Font in the Church at Ngasegalatu, A Column Supporting the Church at Ngasegalatu, The Entrance to the Church at Ngasegalatu* Of this village church built 1935—1937 we have no exterior picture. The church no longer stands. In 20 years it had become dilapidated and was replaced by a new church in 1958. The chief carver was *Dawidi*, who created the seven-branch candelabrum on the altar (left), and the candlestick on the left side of the altar, also the lamb on the pulpit and the carved pillars. The figures on the pillars are supposed to be "ancestral figures," but they now represent their spiritual ancestors: the prophets and the evangelists. At each end of the altar stood a candlestick with one candle each. On the candlestick to the left a human figure may be seen: the representation of an apostle. The baptismal font in front of the altar is painted red (with red chalk) and white (lime). The head above the altar cross represents God, the Creator of heaven and earth. Above that (concealed by the beam) is a carved head of Christ with a crown placed on it.—The pulpit (print 273) reminds one of a canoe and therefore of the fact that Jesus preached from a boat. Since the Jabem people are seafaring, the story makes a strong impression on them. —It is doubtful whether the pillar (print 275) was created by the carver *Dawidi*, as could be supposed. It stands in the interior of the church in front of the pulpit and has the figure of an evangelist on it. The wood carving is painted red and white.—The dove above the entrance (print 276) is not to be understood in this case as a symbol of the Holy Spirit. Here it represents Noah's dove that flew out of the ark. The missionary was given the following explanation: "In like manner the dove here keeps watch to see if peace reigns in the world, especially among those who come to the services."—The dove is so set up that it can be enclosed in the opening behind it (with a string).

277. *Pulpit*
Pastor Akikepe is standing in the wooden pulpit at Ulap (New Guinea). It is fashioned from the trunk of a tree. A roof made of banana leaves serves as protection against the sun.

278. *Altar Painting at Gilang*
New Guinea, 1960.

279. *Altar*
This altar of a Papuan church has been set up in the Mission Museum of Neuendettelsau. On both sides of the altar are grooved and painted carvings on boards. To the right is Mary with the Child, the risen Christ on the left. On the altar is the *Crucifixion* by *Tine Kalai* (print 247); in front of it are candleholders.

280. *Angel*
The figure stands in the chancel of the church at Tape (New Guinea) and was carved by the Papuan Pastor *Eoke* in 1963.

281. *Christ*
This groove-carved creation which represents Christ as the Lord of the world was done by a Papuan teacher and is in the Mission Museum at Neuendettelsau.

282. *Mary*
Wood carving from South Seas area.

Index of Pictures

A. Biblical Themes

B. General Themes

Source of Pictures

Bibliography *

A

1. Abble, A., et al. *Des Prêtres noirs S'Interrogent.* Editions du Cerf. Paris, 1957.

2. *Acta et decreta primi Concilii Planarii Indiae 1950.* Ranchi, 1951. Nos. 352, 353, 355.

3. *Schwarzes Afrika.* Vol. I. Göttingen, 1961.

4. Aggen, Johan B. "Misjonen og Kunsten," *Norsk Tidskrift for Misjon* (1957), 215—19.

5. Alexander, Stella. "The Architecture of Old Goa," *The Illustrated Weekly of India* (Feb. 20, 1955).

6. All-Kenya. "Religious Art Exhibition," *World Christian Education*, XVIII, iv (1963), 128—29.

7. Althaus, Paul. "Die Illustration der Bibel als theologisches Problem," *Neue Zeitschrift für Systematische Theologie*, 1 (1959), 314—26.

8. Ancilla, Sr. "Schwarze Künstlerin," *Die Katholischen Missionen*, LXXVIII (1959), 125—26.

9. *And Was Made Man.* (The Life of Our Lord in Pictures by Students of the Makerere College. Kampala School of Art.) London, 1956.

10. Andresen, Carl. "Altchristliche Kritik am Tanz—ein Ausschnitt aus dem Kampf der alten Kirche gegen heidnische Sitte," *Zeitschrift für Kirchengeschichte*, LXXII (1961), 217—62.

11. Anheuser, Clemens P., O.F.M.: *Missionsgeschichte auf Briefmarken.* Münster, 1962.

12. Antweiler, Anton. "Ägyptische Kunst," *Zeitschrift für Missionswissenschaft und Religionswissenschaft*, XLV (1961), 150—51.

13. Archer, Mildred, and William George. *Indian Painting for the British, 1770—1880.* London, 1955.

14. Arnold, Thomas W. *The Old and New Testaments in Muslim Religious Art.* London, 1932.

15. "Art, Indian Christian." *The Salesian* (Nov. 1942).

* See also the bibliography in Arno Lehmann, *Die Kunst der Jungen Kirchen* (Berlin: Evang. Verlagsanstalt, 1957), pp. 249—53.

16. "Art, Indian Christian." *Messenger of S. Heart* (Nov. 1942).

17. "L'Artisan et les Arts liturgiques. Art chrétien du Congo," *Abbaye de Saint-André-les-Bruges*, XVIII, 4 (1949).

18. *L'Artisan liturgique* (Oct.—Dec. 1936). Prints on pp. 890—91, 914—15, 917.

19. *Arts Liturgical*, XXII (1953), 17, 20—23.

B

20. Baëta, C. G. *Prophetism in Ghana.* London, 1962.

21. Bahr, Hans-Eckehard. *Poiesis. Theologische Untersuchung der Kunst.* Stuttgart, 1961.

22. Indian Ballet. *World Christian Education*, XVIII, 1 (1963), 23.

23. Beaver, R. Pierce. "New Patterns in Missions." Mimeographed report on the Lutheran Foreign Missions Conference, Buck Hill Falls, Pa., Nov. 1962.

24. *Beier*, H. U. "Christliche Kunst in Nigeria," *Frankfurter Allgemeine Zeitung* (Dec. 21, 1957).

25. Beier, Ulli. *Art in Nigeria.* London, 1960.

26. Berndt, Manfred. "Adaption of the Religious Dance and Similar Physical Movements in the Indigenous Church." Mimeographed diss., Concordia Seminary, St. Louis, Mo. (1961).

27. Beurdeley, M. Michel. *Porcelaine de la Compagnie des Indes.* Fribourg. Office du livre (1962).

28. "Bible Pictures as Painted by a Northfield Student in the Style of Ancient Chinese," *St. Paul Sunday Pioneer Press* (1957), 10, 12—13.

29. *Bibliografia Missionaria*, 25 (1962). (This bibliography lists also all literature on art.)

30. Biéler, André. *Liturgie et Architecture. Le Temple des Chrétiens.*

31. Blaser, Werner. *Tempel und Teehaus in Japan.* Olten, Lausanne, 1955.

32. Bornemann, Fritz. "Ars sacra Pekinensis. Die chinesisch-christliche Malerei an der katholischen Universität (Fu Jen) in Peking." Mödling bei Wien, 1950.

33, Boyd, Ernest. *The Literature of Santos.* Dallas, Tex.

34. Briault, R. P. *L'Architecture au Pays de Mission.* Paris, 1938.

35. Bühlmann, Walbert. *Afrika*, Mainz, 1963. Pp. 112, 217, 218—22.

36. Bürkle, Horst. "Kirchenbau in Übersee," *Kunst und Kirche*, XXV (1962), 81—87.

37. Bürkler, Xaver. "Katechismus-Illustrationen in China. Chinesische Stimmen zur christlichen chinesischen Kunst," *Neue Zeitschrift für Missionswissenschaft*, XXXVI (1952), 294—301.

38. *Building Project of Yamato Christian Church.* Kyoto (Japan), no date.

39. Burckhardt, Titus. *Vom Wesen heiliger Kunst in den Weltreligionen.* Zurich, 1955.

40. Butler, John F. "Christian Art Overseas," *The Congregational Quarterly*, XXXIV (1956), 154—61.

41. —. "Can Missions Rescue Modern Art?" *The Hibbert Journal*, LVI (1958), 377—87.

42. —. "Nineteen Centuries of Christian Missionary Architecture," *Journal of Architectural Historians*, XXI (1962), 3—17.

43. —. "Christ in Ivory," *The Methodist Magazine* (March 1961), 86—89.

44. —. Culture-Minglings in Human Relations and International Obligations. A Report of the Unesco-Indian Philosophical Congress, Held at Ceylon, December 1954. Bangalore, 1956. Pp. 115—25.

45. —. "The Dilemma of Religious Art," *The Philosophical Quarterly*, XXX (1957), 159—64.

46. —. "Modernist Art in the Younger Churches," *Wort und Antwort. Festschrift für Arno Lehmann.* Halle, 1961 (mimeographed).

47. —. A review of Arno Lehmann, *Die Kunst der Jungen Kirchen*, in *International Review of Missions*, XLV (1956), 467—68.

48. —. "The Theology of Church Building in India," *The Indian Journal of Theology*, V (1956), 1—20.

49. —. "Further Thoughts on Church Architecture in India," ibid., VIII (1959), 135—50.

C

50. Cali, François. *Kunst der Konquistadoren.* Paris, 1960.

51. Campbell, J. McLeod. *A Singhalese Chapel for Trinity College, Kandy.* Kandy, 1926.

52. Campenhausen, Hans Frhr. von. "Die Bilderfrage in der Reformation," *Zeitschrift für Kirchengeschichte*, LXVIII (1957), 96—128.

53. Camps, Arnulf. "The Influence of Western Art." In "Jerome Xavier S. J. and the Muslims of the Mogul Empire," *Nouvelle Revue de Science Missionaire* (1957), 202—10.

54. Carrol, L. Kevin. "Christian Art in Africa," *African Ecclesiastical Review* (1961).

55. —. "Art from the Soul of Nigeria," *World Mission*, V (1955), 307—19.

56. —. "Ist christlich-afrikanische Kunst möglich?" *Die Katholischen Missionen*, LXXX (1961), 191—96.

57. *Catalogue* (illustr.) *of the Vatican Exhibition of Missionary Art.* Rome, 1950.

58. Chandran, J. Russell. "Christian Art in Africa," *Overseas News*, No. 80 (Aug. 4, 1948).

59. —. "Christ of the Indian Road," ibid., p. 3.

60. —. "The Church in and against it's Cultural Environment," *International Review of Missions*, XLI (1952), 257—72.

61. Chiang Yee. *The Chinese Eye.* London, 1960[4].

62. "A Chinese Paints the Story of Christmas," *St. Paul Sunday Pioneer Press* (Dec. 6—7, 1956).

63. "Christ Appears as a Plain Indian in Paintings by Cherokee Artist," *The Kansas City Times* (April 19, 1957).

64. Christoffels, Hildegard. "Zur Methodik des Studiums exotischer Kunst," *Neue Zeitschrift für Missionswissenschaft*, XVI (1960), 222—25.

65. "Catholic Church in Indian Style," *Times of India* (July 23, 1934).

66. "Indian Church Style," *Clergy Monthly*, V, 210.

67. Cieslek, Hubert, S.J. "Kirishitan-Kunst," *Neue Zeitschrift für Missionswissenschaft*, VIII (1952), 97—104, 161—77.

68. Clarke, Basil Fulford Lowther. *Anglican Cathedrals outside the British Isles*. London, 1958.

69. The Commission on Christian Literature of the Methodist Church in Southern Asia, ed. *Christian Art in India*. Lucknow, U. P., no date.

70. Constantini, Celso. *L'Art chrétien dans les Missions*. Paris, 1949—50.

71. —. *L'arte cristiana nelle missioni*. Rome, 1940.

72. —. *L'istruzione del S. Offizio sull' arte sacra*. Rome, 1952.

73. —. *La Madonna nella nuova arte missionaria*. Edizioni della Pontificia Commissione Centrale per l'arte sacra. Rome (1956), Reprint as *Fede e Arte*.

74. —. "Il pittore Angela da Fonseca," *Arte cristiana* (Aug. 1938).

75. —. "Rinascimento dell' arte missionaria," *Missionswissenschaftliche Studien. Festgabe, Prof. Dr. Joh. Dindinger . . . zum 70. Lebensjahre dargeboten. . . .* Aachen, 1951.

76. "Cyrene und seine Kunst," *Reformierte Schweiz*, XV (1958), 82—86.

D

77. Damant, G. *Samuel Makoanyane*. Morija (Basutoland), 1951.

78. Danusaputro, R. S. "Munadjat: Indonesische Musik," *Die Katholischen Missionen*, LXXV (1956), 175—77.

79. Dark, Philipp. "The Art of Africa, III: West African Bronzes," *Africa South*, III, 2 (1959), 109—16.

80. "Daß religiöse Kunst und Literatur in den Missionen in würdiger und fruchtbarer Weise gefördert werden," *Herder-Korrespondenz*, 16 (1961—62), 400—401.

81. Dayakishor. "The Catholic Church and Indian Culture," *World Mission* IV, 1 (1953), 13—24.

82. Decker, Hanna, "Afrikanischer Kreuzweg," *Die Katholischen Missionen*, LXXIX (1960), 69—70.

83. Devanesen, Chandran. *The Cross Is Lifted*. New York, 1954.

84. "For the Development of Native Art," *Clergy Monthly*, VI, 129.

85. Diego, F. "On the Building of Churches," *Collecteana Punjabensia*, 1951, p. 386.

86. —. "Catholic Mission or European Settlement," ibid., 1950, pp. 257ff., 284ff.

87. Drake, Edith M. "Image and Symbol. Teaching the Bible through Drama," *World Christian Education*, XVIII, 3 (1963), 93—94.

88. Drinkwaters, F. H. "La Réligion enseignée par de Drame," *Lumen Vitae*, III (1948), 154—72.

E

89. Eklundh, Bernt. "Konst fran de unga Kyrkorna," *Kristet forum*, III (April 1960), 64—67.

90. d'Elia, Pasquale M. *Le origini dell' arte cristiana Cinese (1583—1640)*. Rome, 1939.

91. Elisofon, Eliot (photography); William Fagg (text). *The Sculpture of Africa*. London, 1958.

92. Ellenberger, John D. "The Beginnings of Hymnology in a New Guinea Church," *Practical Anthropology*, IX, 6 (1962), 263—67.

93. Elliger, Walter. *Die Stellung der alten Christen zu den Bildern in den ersten vier Jahrhunderten*. Leipzig, 1930 (studies on Christian monuments, 20).

94. *Der große Entschluß*, X, (Feb. 1954—55), Table VI.

95. Erkes, Eduard. "Ein chinesisch-katholisches Heiligenbild," *Jahrbuch des Museums für Völkerkunde zu Leipzig*, XV (1956), 31—36.

96. Exhibition of Christian Art in India, October 31 to November 9, 1956 (catalogue). Lucknow (India), 1956.

F

97. Finbar, Fr. "Indian Christian Art," *Collecteana Punjabensia*, 1949, p. 191.

98. Fleming, Daniel Johnson. *Heritage of Beauty*. New York, 1937.

99. Fonseca, Angelo da. "Indo-Christian Art in Painting and Statuary," *Indica. The Indian Historical Research Institute. Silver Jubilee. Commemoration Vol. St. Xavier's College*. Bombay, 1953.

100. —. "Indian Christian Art. In Historical Retrospect," *Indica*. Bombay, 1948.

101. —. "Reasons for Integration of Indian Artistic Heritage in the Liturgical Arts," *Wort und Antwort. Festschrift für Arno Lehmann*. Halle, 1961 (mimeographed).

102. *Architectural Forum* (Dec. 1955).

103. Foster, John. "Christian Art in Fourteenth-Century China," *International Review of Missions*, LI (1962), 430—38.

104. —. "Christian Art Forms from Fourteenth-Century China," *Wort und Antwort. Festschrift für Arno Lehmann*. Halle, 1961 (mimeographed).

105. —. "Crosses and Angels from Fourteenth-Century China," *International Review of Missions*, XLIV (1955), 170—74.

106. —. "Crosses from the Walls of Zaitun," *Journal of the Royal Asiatic Society* (April 1954), 1—25 (16 prints).

107. Freitag, Anton. *Die Wege des Heils. Bildatlas zur Geschichte der Weltmission.* Salzburg, 1960.

108. Freuler, Karl. "Die neue Kathedrale in Tokyo," *Die Katholischen Missionen,* LXXXII (1963), 44—45.

109. —. "Vom Kirchenbauen in der Mission," ibid., LXXVIII (1959), 171—74.

110. Fry, Roger Eliot. "Les Peintres de Poto-Poto," *Katholisches Missionsjahrbuch der Schweiz* (1962), pp. 46—48.

111. —. *Vision and Design.* Harmondsworth, 1937 (Pelican Books, A 20).

G

112. Geraert, Fr. A. "Indian Church," *Our Field* (Kurseon), (1926), H. 2, 125—27; (1927), H. 3, 27.

113. —. "For Developing a Native Art," *Clergy Monthly,* VI, 238.

114. Gibson, J. P. S. R. "A Christian Sinhalese Artist," *C. M. S. Outlook* (May 1938), 100—102.

115. *Glaube und Bild. Der Bildhauer Albert Wider. Zum 50. Geburtstag des Künstlers.* Widnau, 1960.

116. Goetz, H. "Some European Influences on Indian Art in the XVII. and XVIII. Centuries," *The New Review* (Calcutta), (1939), 139—44.

117. Goldammer, Kurt. "Frühchristliche Kunst als Missionskunst," *Wort und Antwort. Festschrift für Arno Lehmann.* Halle, 1961 (mimeographed).

118. Goodwin, A. J. H. "The Art of Africa. An Introduction," *Africa South,* II, 4 (1958), 94—101.

119. Graf, Ursula. "Das Weihnachtsbild bei fremden Völkern," *Nürnberger Zeitung* (1957), 12, 19, 21.

120. Grossmann, Rudolf: "Der geistige Umbruch im lateinischen Amerika," *Lutherische Rundschau,* XI (1961), 265—77.

121. Gurney-Champion, Margaret. "Joy in the Church," *C. M. S. Outlook* (March 2—3, 1961).

H

122. Haselberger, Herta. "Wandmalereien und plastischer Bauschmuck in Guinea," *Jahrbuch des Museums für Völkerkunde zu Leipzig,* XIX (1962), 138—66.

123. Heim, Walter. "Bemühungen um den eigenständigen Kirchengesang in Japan und Afrika," *Heiliger Dienst* (1963), pp. 69—71.

124. Heinz, Karl Malte. "Religious Architecture in India," *Liturgical Arts* (Nov. 1963).

125. Heras, Fr. R. "Indian Art in Catholic Churches," *The Examiner* (1927), pp. 474, 488, 501.

126. —. "A Catholic Church in Indian Style," *Liturgical Arts,* I (1935), 43.

127. —. "The Church and India," *The Examiner* (1938), p. 321.

128. Hestermann, Ferdinand. "Zur Analyse der abendländischen und ostasiatischen Baukunde," *Wissenschaftliche Zeitschrift der Friedrich-Schiller-Universität Jena,* III (1953—54), *Ges. u. sprachw. Reihe,* 191—200.

129. Hobler, Friedrich. "Indisch-christliche Kunst. Gespräch mit Angelo da Fonseca," *Die Katholischen Missionen,* LXXIV (1955), 173—75.

130. Höltker, Georg. "Missionskunst als Problem und Aufgabe," *Neue Zeitschrift für Missionswissenschaft,* XIX (1963), 228—29.

131. Hofinger, Johannes. "Missionskatechetische Bedeutung und rechte Gestaltung des religiösen Schauspiels. Unter besonderer Berücksichtigung der chinesischen Mission," *Zeitschrift für Missionswissenschaft und Religionswissenschaft,* XXXVII (1953), 320—24.

132. —. *Worship: The Life of the Missions.* Notre Dame, Ind., 1958.

133. Hoh-Peh, Monika Liu. "Ich male für Gott," *Die Katholischen Missionen,* LXXIV (1955), 135—138.

134. Hosten, H. *Antiquities from San Thomé and Mylapare.* Mylapare, 1936.

135. "How to Foster Indian Christian Art," *Clergy Monthly,* VII, 209.

136. Huber, F. "Afrikanische Kirchengeschichte im Spiegel der Markenbilder," *Afrika 1960,* pp. 41ff.

137. Hürtgen, Basilissa. *Sakraler Tanz (neue Versuche), Zeitchrift für Missionswissenschaft und Religionswissenschaft,* XLI (1957), 193—200.

I

138. "Image and Symbol: Search for an Indigenous Christian Art: Thailand," *World Christian Education,* XVIII, 1 (1963), 23—32.

139. Immoos, Thomas S. M. B. "Wege und Irrwege der Missionsarchitectur," *Die Katholischen Missionen,* LXXXII (1963), 46—49.

140. *India* (postcard). Rome: Central Committee of the Holy Year, Vatican Exhibition.

141. Italiaander, Rolf. *Neue Kunst in Afrika.* Mannheim, 1957.

142. —. *Tanz in Afrika.* Berlin, 1960.

J

143. Jäger, Otto Arnold. *Äthiopische Miniaturen.* Berlin, 1957.

144. Jahn, Janheinz. *Muntu. Umrisse der neoafrikanischen Kultur.* Düsseldorf, 1958 (American: New York, 1961; English: London, 1961; French: Paris, 1961; Italian: Turin, 1961; Swedish: Stockholm, 1960).

145. Jerome, Fr. "Our Religious Statuary," *Clergy Monthly,* VI, 194.

146. Jones, J. Ffranggoon. "Religious Patronage—Cyrene," *Africa South,* II, 4 (1958), 106—108.

147. Jones, Richard M. *Manual for Witness through the Arts.* Valley Forge, Pa., 1961.

148. Jergensen, K. E. Jordt. "Bibel og Billede," *Kirkens Verden*, II (1960), 16—25.

149. Joseph, T. K. *Malabar Christians and Their Ancient Documents*. Trivandrum, 1929.

150. *International Journal of Religious Education* (a special issue: "Art in Christian Education") XXXV, 4 (1959).

K

151. Kagame, Alexis. "Ein schwarzer 'Heiland'," *Die Katholischen Missionen*, LXXVI (1957), 35—38.

152. Key, Mary. "Hymn Writing with Indigenous Tunes," *Practical Anthropology*, IX, 4 (1962), 257—62.

153. Khandalavaivala, Karl. "Indian Art Yesterday and Today," *The Atlantic* (Oct. 1950).

154. King, Louis L. "Indigenous Hymnody of the Ivory Coast," *Practical Anthropology*, IX, 4 (1962), 268—71.

155. *Evangelische Kirchenbautagung. Kirchenbau und Ökumene*, ed. Gerhard Langmaack. Hamburg, 1962, pp. 85ff., 97ff.

156. Kubler, George, and Martin Sebastian Soria. *Art and Architecture in Spain and Portugal and Their American Dominions. 1500 to 1800*. Harmondsworth, 1959.

157. Kunst, Jaap. *De Inheemsche Muziek en de Zending*. Amsterdam, 1947.

158. "Kunst, Kult Kontinente," *Katholisches Missionsjahrbuch der Schweiz*, 1962.

159. "Papuanische Kunst," *In alle Welt*, XIII, 5 (1961), 75—76.

L

160. La Dany, Ladislaus. "Asien ohne Klischee," *Wort und Wahrheit*, XVIII (1963), 25—33.

161. Laufer, Carl. "Einheimisch bauen wir die Kirche," *Die Katholischen Missionen*, LXXX (1961), 89—92.

162. —. "Fehlbeurteilung der Eingeborenenpsyche in der Südseemission," *Neue Zeitschrift für Missionswissenschaft*, XV (1959), 51—59.

163. Lautenschlager, Georg. "Kirchliche Negerkunst in Südafrika," *Zeitschrift für Missionswissenschaft und Religionswissenschaft*, XLII (1958), 331.

164. Lavanoux, Maurice. "Christian Art Trends in Asia," *World Mission*, III (1953), 101—102.

165. Layman. "Liturgy and Art in India," *Clergy Monthly*, VII, 209.

166. Leeuw, Gerard van der. *Vom Heiligen in der Kunst*. Gütersloh, 1957³.

167. Legum, Colin, ed. *Africa: A Handbook to the Continent*. New York, 1962 (aspects of African art).

168. Lehmann, Arno. "Andere malen anders—ökumenische Kunst," *Der Staedtler-Brief*, 1961, H. 6, 140—41, 144.

169. —. "Art for Asia's Sake," ed. Frances Bonwick, *As Asia Goes*. Toronto, 1962, pp. 104—14.

170. —. "Indigenous Art and Bible-Illustration," *Wissenschaftliche Zeitschrift der Martin-Luther-Universität Halle-Wittenberg. Ges. u. sprachw. Reihe*, IX (1960), 123—35. Also in *Occasional Bulletin from the Missionary Research Library*, XII (1961), 1—9.

171. —. "Les Artistes des Jeunes Églises," *L'Illustré Protestant*, VII (1959), 14—17.

172. —. "Derselbe Christus," *Die Zeichen der Zeit*, XV (1961), 108—11.

173. —. "Kirchenbau VII: In den Missionsgebieten und in den jungen Kirchen," *RGG³*, III, 1410—11.

174. —. "An der Krippe des Weltheilands," *Missionsblatt der Evang.-Luth. Freikirchen*, LIII (1961), 230—35.

175. —. "Afro-asiatische Kunst und Bibelillustration," *Evangelische Missionszeitschrift* (1960), 33—44.

176. —. "Die Kunst der anderen," *Kirchenbote* (1957), 26—29.

177. —. "Die Kunst der anderen," Lehmann, Joachim, ed. *Festschrift zum 75. Geburtstag von Prof. E. Hahs* (1962) (mimeographed).

178. —. "Malerei und Plastik VII: Christliche Kunst in den jungen Kirchen," *RGG³*, IV, 702—704.

179. —. "Indische Kunst," Meyer, Heinrich, eds. *Wir lieben Indien*. Salzuflen, 1963, pp. 257—64.

180. —. *Die Kunst der Jungen Kirchen*. Berlin, 1955, 1957².

181. —. "Kunst der Jungen Kirchen," *Weltkirchenlexikon*, 811—13.

182. —. "Kunst der Ökumene, *Christlicher Hauskalender*, 1956, pp. 56—60.

183. —. "Aus der Kunst der Ökumene," Freytag, Walter, und Hans Jürgen Schultz: *Evangelische Weihnacht*, Series 9. Hamburg, 1956, pp. 172—75.

184. —. "Kunst in tausend Sprachen," *Neue Zeit*, XXV (1959), 12.

185. —. "Stedegen Kristan Kunst om Nasjonal Bibel-illustration," *Norsk Tidskrift for Misjon*, XIV (1960), 65—79.

186. —. "Unbekannte afroasiatische Kunst," *Forschungen und Fortschritte*, XXXV (1961), 91—93. Also in *Lutherische Blätter*, XIII (1962), 42—47.

187. —. "Mit anderen Pinseln gemalt," *Missionsplatz der Evang.-Luth. Freikirchen*, L (1958), 208—10.

188. —. "Mit welchem Pinsel?" *Deutsches Pfarrerblatt*, LX (1960), 29—31. Also "With Which Brush?" *Practical Anthropology*, VII (1960), 253—55.

189. —. *Mit anderen Pinseln. Filmstrips with Text*. Radebeul, 1960.

190. —. "Sie haben denselben Christus," *Lutherische Blätter*, XII (1960), 54—61.

191. —. *Weihnachten und Karfreitag in der ökumenischen Kunst. Filmstrips with Text*. Radebeul, 1960.

192. Leiris, Michel. "The African Negroes and the Arts of Carving and Sculpture," *Unity and Diversity of Cultures*, II (1953), 316—52.

193. Lewis, Albert. *Decorative Art of New Guinea. Incised Designs.* Chicago, 1925.

194. *Life of Christ, by Chinese Artists.* London, 1939.

195. Lobo, A. D. "Christian Art in India," *The Examiner* (July 13, 1957), pp. 349—51.

196. Loetscher, Anton. "Schnitzerschule von Serima, *Die Katholischen Missionen,* LXXIX (1960), 84—87.

197. Löwenstein, Felix zu. *Christliche Bilder in altindischer Malerei.* Münster, 1958.

198. Lüthi, Kurt. "Bildende Kunst als theologisches Problem," *Theologische Zeitschrift,* XVI (1960), 120—32.

M

199. Maclagan, Edward Douglas. *The Jesuits and the Great Mogul.* London, 1932 (chap. 15: "The Missions and Mogul Painting," 222—67).

200. *Magazine—Souvenir of the S.S.H.M. 1956 to 1959.* Allahabad, 1959.

201. Malenfant, Jerome. "The C.B.C.I. Commission in Indian Christian Art," *India Missionary Bulletin,* II (1954), 13—14.

202. "Die Malerei in Abessinien," *Globus,* LXXXVI (1904), 327—29.

203. Masasi, Vincent. "The Arts in the Mission Field: Africa," *The Church Overseas,* IV (Jan. 1931).

204. Maus, Cynthia Pearl. *The Church and the Fine Arts; an Anthology of Pictures, Poetry, Music, and Stories Portraying the Growth and Development of the Church through the Centuries.* New York, 1960.

205. McIntire, Robert, and Richard Irwin, "Religious Art in Brazil," *Sight-Souns,* XI, 1 (1963), 7—8.

206. Meersman, Achilles. *Franciscans in Bombay. History of the Franciscans in the Territory Comprised within the Boundaries of the Present Archidiocese of Bombay.* Bangalore, 1957.

207. "Messis. Schweizerische katholische Missionsausstellung 1955." Bibliography in *Katholisches Missionsjahrbuch der Schweiz,* XXIII (1956), 6ff., 14ff., 85.

208. Meulder, E. de. "Kunstapostolaat in Indie," *Kerk en Missie 1928,* pp. 149—54.

209. Meylemans. "Noodzakelijkheid van aanpassing der negerkunst in de afrikaanse kerken," *De Bode van Engelendale* (1947), No. 6, pp. 78—81.

210. Michalson, Carl. *Japanische Theologie der Gegenwart,* Gütersloh, 1962.

211. Mills, Edward David. *The Modern Church.* London, 1956.

212. Ministère du Nord Canadien et des Resources Nationales, ed. *L'Art Esquimau au Canada,* Ottawa, 1963.

213. Monchanin, Jules et Henri le Saux. *Die Eremiten von Saccidânanda.* Salzburg, 1962.

214. Moore, James J. "Television Serving Korea's Churches," *World Christian Education* (1963), No. 3, pp. 91—92.

215. General Catalogue, "Mostra d'arte missionaria." Rome: Central Committee of the Holy Year. Vatican Exhibition.

216. "Murals in a Bombay Chapel," *The Illustrated Weekly of India* (April 10, 1955), 40—41.

217. Murray, K. C. "West African Wood Carving," *Africa South,* II, 4 (1958), 102—105.

N

218. Nathan, Walter Ludwig. *Art and the Message of the Church.* Philadelphia, 1961.

219. "Negerkunst und Christentum. Ausstellung März/April 1957 in der Städtischen Kunsthalle Recklinghausen, durch das Holländische Katholische Missionsinstitut. Einführung von F. van Trigt" (catalogue).

220. Neuner, Josef, S.J. "Die Weltkirche. Die Katholizität der Kirche im Missionswerk," Holböck, Ferdinand, and Thomas Sartory, O.S.B., eds. *Mysterium Kirche in der Sicht der theologischen Disziplinen* II. Salzburg, 1962, pp. 815—89.

221. Nishimura, Tei. *Namban Art. Christian Art in Japan 1549—1639.* Kodansha, 1958.

222. Njau, E. P. *Art Master's Hobby* (catalog). Makerere, 1962.

223. —. "Let the Children Paint." An Exhibition of Art in Various Media, The Sorsbie Gallery, April—May 1962 (catalogue). Makarere: Makarere University College Library, 1962.

224. —. "Every Man an Artist," *Rock* (March 3, 1963).

225. Njau, Elimo. "Copying Puts God to Sleep. Some Thoughts on the True African and Art," *Transition* III, 9 (1963), 15—17.

226. Nketia, J. H. "The Contribution of African Culture to Christian Worship," *International Review of Missions,* XLVII (1958), 265—78.

227. Northrop, C. *The Meeting of East and West.* New York, 1953.

228. Nuoffer, Oskar. *Afrikanische Plastik in der Gestaltung von Mutter und Kind.* Dresden, 1925.

O

229. Oehler, W. "Marienkult und Kwanjinverehrung in der chinesischen Kunst," *Deutsches Pfarrerblatt,* LIV (1954), 508—10.

230. Ohm, Thomas, O.S.B. "Die Ars-Sacra-Ausstellung der Missionsländer in Rom," *Anno Santo* (1950), 570—71.

231. —. *Ex contemplatione loqui.* Münster, 1961.

232. —. "Over Heiligdommen en Liturgische Plaatsen in de Missiegebieden," *Tijdschrift voor Liturgie,* XXXIV (1950), 250—60.

233. —. *Das Katechumenat in den katholischen Missionen.* Münster, 1961.

234. —. "Kirchenbaukunst in Korea," *Werkblätter* (1938), No. 11, pp. 27—35.

235. —. *Machet zu Jüngern alle Völker.* Freiburg i. Br., 1962, 586ff. (Index: Art, p. 903, Pictures, p. 893).

236. —. "Vom Malen, Zeichnen und Lernen in den Missionen," *Zeitschrift für Missionswissenschaft und Religionswissenschaft,* XLIV (1960), 63—64.

237. —. *Asiens Nein und Ja zum westlichen Christentum.* München, 1960², pp. 193—97.

238. Okae, J. D. "Einheimische christliche Kunst in Ghana," *Der Auftrag* (Sept.—Oct. 1963), 106—108.

239. Olbrechts, Frans M. *Plastiek van Kongo.* Antwerp, Brussels, Ghent, Louvain, 1946.

240. Olichon, Armand Louis. *Father Six, Parish Priest and Viceroy. . . .* London, 1954.

241. Orthbandt, Eberhard, und Dietrich Hans Teuffen. *Ein Kreuz und tausend Wege.* Constance, 1962.

242. Otto, Jos. A. "Ein Flame malt chinesisch," *Die Katholischen Missionen,* LXIX (1950), 42—47.

243. Overath, Johannes, ed. *IV. Internationaler Kongress für Kirchenmusik in Köln. 22.—30. Juni 1961. Dokumente und Berichte.* Cologne, 1962.

P

244. Parsons, Esther C. *Isleta Paintings.* Washington, 1962.

245. Parsons, Robert T. *The Churches and Ghana Society 1918—1955.* Leiden, 1963.

246. *Afrikanische Passion.* Introduction by John Taylor. Munich, 1957; Berlin, 1964.

247. "A Passion Play in Ahmedabad," *The Illustrated Weekly of India* (June 22, 1958), 36—38.

248. Peel, Joyce M. "Developing Opportunities for Religious Drama in India Today," *International Review of Missions,* LI (1962), 466—70.

249. — and Darius L. Swann. *Drama for the Church. A Handbook on Religious Drama.* Madras, 1962.

250. "About Indian Pictures," *India Missionary Bulletin,* I (1953), 205—209.

251. Pientia, M., Sr. CPS. "Church Art and Architecture in the Missions," Desmond J. Hatton in *Missiology in Africa Today.* Dublin, 1961, pp. 108—14.

252. Pilhofer, Georg. *Die Geschichte der Neuendettelsauer Mission in Neuguinea III.* Neuendettelsau, 1962.

253. Playne, Beatrice. *St. George for Ethiopia.* London, 1954.

254. First Plenary Council of India. Decr. Nos. 355, 356.

255. Preuss, Horst Dietrich, *Maria bei Luther.* Gütersloh, 1954 (*Schriften des Vereins für Reformationsgeschichte 172*).

256. "Haitian Primitives Speak from Cathedral Walls," *Forth* (March 21—23, 1957).

257. "The Problem of Indian Christian Art," *Clergy Monthly Suppl.* (Dec. 1956), p. 139.

258. Proksch, Fr. G. *Kristayan* (Hindi Life of Christ).

R

259. Rachewiltz, Boris de. *Afrikanische Kunst.* Zürich, 1960.

260. Radshar, A. "A Survey of Missionary Art," *Art Notes* (1954, No. 3).

261. Raman, A. S. "Die moderne Malerei Indiens," *Universitas,* X (1955), 1197—1200.

262. Rannenberg, Werner. "Überkommene Form und eigene Antwort. Das Ringen um eine einheimische Gestalt in den Kirchen Asiens und Afrikas," *Das Wort in der Welt,* XXXIX (1960), 57—62.

263. Rao, Ramachandra. *Modern Indian Painting.* Madras, 1953 (prints 43, 62, 63, 102).

264. Rapp, Urban. *Das Mysterienbild.* Münsterschwarzbach, 1952.

265. —. "Die Neuheit auf dem Gebiete der Kunst" in Laurenz Kilger, *Die Neuheit des Lebens als Ziel und Frucht der Weltmission.* Münster, 1957, pp. 249—65.

266. Raymond, Leonard. "Indische Musik im Dienste der Kirche," *Die Katholischen Missionen,* LXXXI (1962), 183—88.

267. Régamey, Pie-Raymond. *L'Art Sacré au XXᵉ Siècle.* Paris, 1952.

268. Reid, Alice. "The Use and Further Development of an Indigenous Indian Christian Pictorial Art." Dissertation, The Biblical Seminary in New York, 1943.

269. Riccitelli, James M. "Developing Non-Western Hymnody," *Practical Anthropology,* IX, 6 (1962), 241—56.

270. Roetheli, E. W. "Kunst und Kirche in Afrika," *Neue Zürcher Nachrichten,* VI, 3, 10 (1955).

271. Rossmann, Vern. "The Breaking in of the Future. The Problem of Indigenization and Cultural Synthesis," *International Review of Missions,* LII (1963), 129—43.

272. Rowland, B. Jr. *Art in East and West.* Oxford: Harvard University Press, 1955.

S

273. S. Congr. of Propaganda. Letter on Indian Christian Styles, *Clergy Monthly,* VI, 131.

274. *S.S.H.M. Musical Bulletin.* Allahabad, 1960.

275. *St. Michaelskalender 1951.* Kaldenkirchen.

276. Salès, Marc Pierre. "Sur l'Art Haitien," *Katholisches Missionsjahrbuch der Schweiz,* 1962, pp. 37—45.

277. *Sam J. Ntiro.* Harmon Foundation, no date.

278. Schelbert, Georg. "Einheimische Kunst und Bibel-Illustrationen im Protestantismus," *Neue Zeitschrift für Missionswissenschaft,* XVI (1960), 305—309.

279. Schmalenbach, Werner. *Die Kunst Afrikas.* Basel, 1953.

280. Schmidlin, Josef. "Missionskunst in Vergangenheit und Gegenwart," *Zeitschrift für Missionswissenschaft und Religionswissenschaft,* XXVII (1937), 157 to 64.

281. Schöne, Wolfgang, Johannes Kollwitz, and Hans Freiherr von Campenhausen, *Das Gottesbild im Abendland*. Berlin, 1959².

282. Schreyer, Lothar. *Christliche Kunst des 20. Jahrhunderts in der katholischen und protestantischen Welt*. Hamburg, 1959.

283. Schüler, Sepp. "Erste afrikanische Bibelillustrationen," *Die Katholischen Missionen*, LXVI (1938), 15—19.

284. —. "Christliche Eingeborenenkunst in nichtchristlichen Ländern," *Die christliche Kunst*, XXXII (1935—36), 193—215.

285. —. "Christliche Eingeborenenkunst aus aller Welt. Die Missionsschau auf der Pariser Weltausstellung 1937," *Die Katholischen Missionen*, LXV (1937), 243—46.

286. —. "Chinesisches 'Jesuitenporzellan'," *Die Katholischen Missionen*, LXVI (1938), 121—26.

287. —. "Afrikanische Kirchenbaukunst," ibid., LXV (1937), 116—20.

288. —. "Christlich-afrikanische Kunst aus der ersten Kongo-Mission (15.—16. Jahrh.)," ibid., pp. 34—40.

289. —. "Die christliche Kunst in China zur Zeit von P. Adam Schall," ibid., LXIV (1936), 68—73.

290. —. *Christliche Kunst aus fernen Ländern*. Düsseldorf, 1939.

291. —. "Christliche Kunst in heidnischem Land," *Akademische Missionsblätter*, II, 1 (1935), 25—44.

292. —. "Einheimische Kunst im Dienste des Religionsunterrichts in den Missionsländern," *Katholisches Missionsjahrbuch der Schweiz*, V (1938), 71—81.

293. —. "Einheimische Kunst als originale Schöpfung," ibid. (1956), 67—73.

294. —. "Neue christliche Kunst in Japan," *Die Katholischen Missionen*, LXIII (1935), 262—68.

295. —. "Die christliche Kunstausstellung in Leopoldville 1936," ibid., LXV (1937), 11—16.

296. —. "Die christliche Kunstausstellung zu Schanghai 1935," ibid., LXIV (1936), 150—54.

297. —. "Christlich-afrikanisches Kunstgewerbe," ibid., LXV (1937), 160—65.

298. —. "Die 'Chinesische Madonna,' der bedeutendste Fund aus der ersten Missionsperiode in China," ibid., LXIV (1936), 177—83.

299. —. *Marienbilder aus aller Welt*, Kevelaer, 1936.

300. —. "Missions-Paramentik," *Kirchliche Textilkunst 1937*, Bericht 2, 31—54.

301. —. "Die Missionsparamentik und ihre notwendige und richtige Förderung durch den Priester," *Priester und Mission*, XXI (1937), 31—42.

302. —. "Der Priester als Anreger und Schöpfer einheimisch-christlicher Kunst in den Missionsländern," ibid., XX (1936), 83—111.

303. —. "P. Matteo Ricci und die christliche Kunst in China," *Die Katholischen Missionen*, LXIV (1936), 3—8.

304. —. "'Der Tod Goliaths' in javanischen Wajangspielen," ibid., LXIII (1935), 148—52.

305. Schurhammer, Georg. *Der Silberschrein des Hl. Franx Xaver in Goa*, no place, no date.

306. Segy, Ladislaus. "African Art: Its Culture," *Africa Is Here*. Report of the North American Assembly on African Affairs, held at Wittenberg College, Springfield, Ohio, June 16—25, 1952. New York, no date, pp. 111—13.

307. —. *African Sculpture Speaks*. New York, 1955.

308. Selhorst, Pientia, CPS. "Art and the Spreading of the Gospel," *World Mission*, XII, 4 (1961), 56—62.

309. Shand, Jean. "The Adaption of Art Forms and Motifs for Use in the Indigenous Christian Church." Dissertation. New York, 1954 (mimeographed).

310. Shek, Kai-nung. *Sketches of Christ from a Chinese Brush*, in collaboration with Olaf K. Skinsnes. Minneapolis, 1956.

311. "Afrikanische Skulpturen," *Der große Entschluß*, IX (1953—54), 143—44.

312. Smalley, William A. "Music, Church and Ethnocentrism." *Practical Anthropology*, IX, 4 (1962), 272 to 73.

313. Solomon, Raj. "Image and Symbol, Arts of Indians Heart of Faith," *World Christian Education*, XVIII, 4 (1963), 128.

314. Sovik, Edward. "Church Architecture," *DWM News Letter*, No. 9 (Oct. 1958).

315. Staffner, Hans. "Das Christus-Purana," *Die Katholischen Missionen*, LXXVII (1958), 35—40.

316. Steffen, Uwe. "Das Bild als theologisches Problem," *Monatsschrift für Pastoraltheologie*, XLVIII (1959), 364—70.

317. *The Student World*, XLVIII, 2 (1955).

318. Sundkler, Bengt. "Bantu Messiah and White Christ," *Practical Anthropology*, VII (1960), 170—76.

T

319. Takenaka, Masao. "The Arts in Christian Education," *World Christian Education*, XVIII (1963), 116—18.

320. Taylor, John Vernon. "The Development of African Drama for Education and Evangelism," *International Revue of Missions*, XXXIX (1950), 292—301.

321. —, and Dorothea A. Lehmann. *Christians of the Copperbelt*. Toronto, 1961.

322. Tegethoff, Wilhelm M. S. C. "Afrikanische Musik und die Kirche in Afrika," *Zeitschrift für Missionswissenschaft und Religionswissenschaft*, XLVI (1962), 54—58.

323. "A Theology of Christian Art," *Clergy Monthly*, Suppl. (Dec. 1956), 417—18.

324. Thomas, M. M. "Indigenization and the Renaissance of Traditional Culture," *International Review of Missions*, LII (1963), 191—94.

325. *Together*, I, 15 (1957).

326. Van Trigt, F., S. M. A. "Light on Christian Art in Black Africa," *World Mission*, X, 3 (1959), 22—32.

V

327. Väth, Alfons. "Zur Frage eines christlich-indischen Kirchenstils," *Die Katholischen Missionen*, LXIV (1936), 29—31.

328. Volken, H., S.J. "Szenen des Evangeliums im indischen Tanz," *Zeitschrift für Missionswissenschaft und Religionswissenschaft*, XL (1956), 165—66.

W

329. Waldenfels, J. B. "Götterspiel wird Gottesspiel," *Die Katholischen Missionen*, LXXVII (1958), 61—62.

330. —. "Religiöse Musik in Japan," ibid., LXXIX (1960), 159—62.

331. Wallace, W. J. "Hymns in Ethiopia," *Practical Anthropology*, IX, 6 (1962), 271.

332. Wang, C. C. "Angels with Neckties," *The Missionary*, XV, 10 (Dec. 1962), 16—17.

333. *Neue Wege der christlichen Malerei in China* (J. A. Otto), ibid., LXIX (1950), 147—48.

334. "Die Weihnachtsgeschichte in der Kunst der Jungen Kirchen," *Sonntagsspiegel* (Dec. 1954), 8 prints.

335. Weragoda, Sydney. "Indigenous Worship in Ceylon's Churches," *World Christian Education*, I (1966), 10—11.

336. Wicki, Josef. "Gesang und Musik im Dienst der alten indischen Jesuitenmission" (ca. 1542—1580), *Zeitschrift für Missionswissenschaft und Religionswissenschaft*, XLV (1961), 15—30.

337. Wohlrab, Friedel, "'Jesus gehört uns!' Er ist ein Shambala geworden," *Nachrichten aus der Bethel-Mission* (1956), 146—48.

338. *World Christian Education*, II (1960).

Z

339. *Zendings Blad der Ned. Herv. Kerk* (1960), No. 10.

283

Christian expression of faith by African and Asian artists, and to point to the direction of future developments.

The author concentrates on Africa and Asia, though he includes a few examples of Eskimo and Indian work in North America and several illustrations from Central America. He surveys works on painting, wood carving, sculpture, and architecture. He also includes a discussion on poetry, drama, dancing, and music.

The 282 illustrations take the viewer on a global tour. The only one of its kind, this collection of photographs enriches the viewer's understanding of the Christian message as he sees its expression in the cultural forms of many nations. Professor Lehmann makes this treasure of illustrations even more valuable in his helpful comments. He acquaints the reader with the life, background, and development of the individual artist.

The text is an extensive introduction to the stormy history of the art of the younger churches. The conflict with European and overseas influence has resulted in the independent form and character of art in Japan, New Guinea, India, and the various African nations. A detailed bibliography makes rare resources available.

This volume promises to be a standard work for all Christian churches, both Protestant and Catholic, and for the community of art. To date it is the most comprehensive book in its field.